INCARCERATED DAD...

A GANGSTA'S WARNING

David K. Hudson and Erica I. Roby

Order this book online at www.trafford.com
or email orders@trafford.com

Most Trafford titles are also available at major online book retailers.

Printed in the United States of America.

ISBN: 978-1-4907-3264-0 (sc)
ISBN: 978-1-4907-3265-7 (e)

Library of Congress Control Number: 2014906389

Trafford rev. 10/28/2014

Trafford PUBLISHING® **www.trafford.com**
North America & international
toll-free: 1 888 232 4444 (USA & Canada)
fax: 812 355 4082

Incarcerated Dad, the anticipated sequel to the critically acclaimed lucid logic of *Gangsta Rap for the Youth**
* A Five Star Rating on Amazon's Book Review

Dedication

All Praises to The Most High. To my Soul-partner, wife, and friend: You have been and still remain the most loving and supportive woman in my life. Through all the challenges, trials and tribulations your fidelity and tenacity has remained steadfast. Through prayer, love, and devotion you give me the qualities of Heaven on earth. To my granddaughter TaNylah, *the choice* is yours! Your future is so bright. To my daughter, Erica Iris-Denise: Time placed us here. We survived the tears over many years. Through it all . . . with love, we grow!

To My Surrogate Daughters and Sons

It takes our village to raise our child. To my niece Syndi; to my nephews Pteris and Sabien Hudson; to Daronique, Darnysus, Devarone; to KaShyra, Keith, and Iviana.

Programs and Organizations

To the El-Hajj Malik El-Shabazz Academy, Lansing, Michigan: May you become the "90-90-90 school" you are striving to be; that's 90% minority, 90% of students eligible for free and reduced-price lunches, and 90% of students deemed proficient on statewide assessment tests—To Chance For Life, Inc. (CFL); Tom Adams and Jessica Taylor: "The Power Circle"—To The Greyhound Inmate Experience (T.G.I.E.)—To Ron and Gaye-Ann: Thank you for rescuing retired greys and for allowing me to socialize and train them.—To Youth Initiative Neighborhood Service Organization, C.A.P.S., Inc., Fathers Incarcerated Needing to be Dad (F.I.N.D. Inc.), Children of Parents Incarcerated, (C.O.P-I), Detroit—To ex-offender programs CeaseFire in Chicago, Safe Streets in Baltimore, and Save Our Streets in New York. *Ain't no stoppin' us now. We're on the move.*

DAILY AFFIRMATION

TODAY WILL BE THE BEST DAY of my life! It will be a day where I honor my ancestors and my parents by doing excellent work. It will be a day of peace while I perform all of my assignments without causing confusion in my classroom, my neighborhood, on campus, or in my surrounding communities.

It will also be a day where I recognize the contributions of all people, especially those of African descent.

Above all, it will be a day where I honor myself by staying focused on my dream of becoming a successful person—by any means necessary!

Excerpts taken from the El-Hajj Malik El-Shabazz Academy, Lansing, Michigan

In Memory of . . .

My big brother Gregory Lynn Hudson: You are my inspiration. Even in the dark, you said I would shine bright. It's all on me now. I miss you, "G."

Mrs. Aleasie Perryman (Zynobia and Stanley's mom): Thanks for being my second mom in my youth. My future is so bright but my past is so ugly. Gone too soon!

David

Auntee Wyma Jean Warren, my great aunt, supporter, and role model. Your master's degree in nursing will be my inspiration to maintain the family tradition in medicine. You have shown me that *Love is more inclusive than the moment or the day.*

Erica Iris

Contents

Preface

I HAVE SPENT THREE DECADES WATCHING YOUNG men come in and out of prison. In many instances these youth accept the prison experience as a rite of passage to manhood. They have the idea that being convicted of a felony and sentenced to a correctional facility certifies their street credit and gives them permission to return to society as an honored street soldier. This is a fallacy of a subculture that is destroying generations of African-American families as well as diminishing the foundation of our society.

Experiencing prison life and seeing our youths come into the system without any positive male role models to imitate, I am inspired to write the second installment in the *Gangsta Rap* trilogy and share the untold stories of this subculture—the things you will not hear on inner city streets, in drug houses, in the news, at board meetings, in neighborhood barbershops or beauty salons, in school, at church, in college, in the temple, or in the many other places people gather.

Understanding that most inner city and rural area youths lack the examples of positive male role models, I've watched the cycle of male-hood continue to perpetuate itself as these young men come into the prison system boasting of fathering several children by different young ladies without any consideration or means for supporting their children. They continue to brag about returning to society and impregnating more unsuspecting girls with the intentions of not accepting the responsibility of traditional fatherhood.

It is of utmost importance that we fully grasp just how critical this trend is to the destruction of our entire culture. It's having a greater negative impact on our community than any war, past forced servitude, or street drugs could ever have. It is a mindset that must be corrected and never accepted. Every man has a duty to choose to accept responsibility for a youth whether he's the biological parent or not. It is our obligation to be part of the village to raise every child to be a productive citizen. The *Gangsta* series is just a portion of my choices as a reformed felon to dispel this delusional rite of passage. What will your choice be?

INTRODUCTION

LET ME RAP TO YOU—FORGET WHAT you heard!

This is not Hollywood! There are no directors, actors, scripts, prison officials, deputies, guards, censors, or cameras. This is just plain real, raw experiences of prison life.

If you think it's all guts, goons, and glory, then think again. It's much more than you've been led to believe. Tell me, do you wanna feel what I'm feeling?

If so, these pages will reveal the side of prison life that is not shown on television or portrayed in the media. It isn't told through the eyes of a news reporter or the lens of a camera. These gangsta tales are direct real-life experiences that you will at some point go through in your life if you think crime, guns, and street hustling are the solution to your anger, your financial problems, manhood, neighborhood beefs, or family history, or are just plain exciting to you. When the judge's gavel drops and the prison sentence is handed down, you will feel what I'm feeling.

For all those who may not physically travel through the prison system's hall of learning, do not for one second believe you are exempt from "the experience."

When you see that single parent with her children struggling to make it another day because the children's father is in prison; when crime rates in your neighborhood increase due to the decline in school enrollment; when fatherless teens run out of control for lack of male role models in your community; when children are being molested by their spiritual teachers or athletic coach; when the stock broker you trusted steals your life savings, or the 401(k) plan in which your employer invested your retirement funds gets swindled—all of these are indications that you may feel the prison experience.

It is the experience that the average parolee or ex-con may not publicly share with you. Because expressing the anguish and heartache he/she has experienced may give an impression of weakness or vulnerability, these emotions go unspoken upon release.

In *Incarcerated Dad: A Gangsta's Warning*, you will get it raw and in-depth from many aspects. There isn't a single course map or clear journey to the minutes, hours, days, and years of pain and suffering in the prison experience. Every hour can bring a different facet of mental anguish, physical injury, or shame in the experience.

The lessons shared are real, raw, and reeling. Learn them from this book or continue your criminal activities and take the prison trek for yourself. I must inform you, if you choose the latter, a prison cell awaits your arrival and the side order of "the experience" increases the price *you* will pay. Shall we allow "the experience" to begin?

"The Courier"
David K. Hudson

THE LUXURY TAX ON CRIME

YOUR INITIAL LUXURY TAX FOR ENTRY into prison is forfeiture of your street symbols. You will be provided with affordable jewels: platinum-plated handcuffs, leg irons, and belly chains. Not ideal bling, bling, huh? Oh, but it's free, like your robbery. No monetary stress 4 U.

Your choice in clothing and jewelry has been selected for you by the state's wardrobe specialist, prison industries. You won't have to worry about street hustling for those T.R.U. Religion or Red Monkey jeans, Air Nike tennis shoes, or Gucci polos. State blue shirts and pants with orange stripes will be provided for you. No need to worry about whether someone else has the same outfit as yours; *everyone* wears the same attire. You're state property now they got you, playa!

In addition, an all-paid-expenses trip to lands far away from your hood is included in the initial tax. The "hood" or "block" you been rep'in, willing to put your life down for, is of no significance in "the experience."

Your neighborhood becomes a distant memory after the judge sentences you. No one tells you it will be quite a while before you see your hood again, if ever.

Oh, did I mention that the travel menu is cold bologna with soiled bread and cheese, maybe? So sit back, enjoy the chauffeur-driven cruise with leg irons forcing your feet and ankles close, hands clinched in your new jewelry, chained around your waist with a lovely black box attached to assure a tight fit.

You will arrive at "the big house" you've always had street dreams of acquiring. Just not quite how you imagined it!

South, up-north, mid-state are areas of your region you never knew existed. Rural, farm, and swamp lands converted into prisons especially designed for your criminal behavior await your arrival. Your block-oriented thinking never achieved the global or universal scale you had the potential to reach. But now, "the experience" has forced you to see how small your thoughts and goals were. Your new travels are much longer than your block thinking of whether your drug money was proper or whether "the bag" was tied tight. Those things don't matter now that you realize genocide was "you ridin' on your own kind" (gang banging).

Prison trips help you understand you weren't thinking right at all. The scenery on the three-to-five hour drive on the state highway up north will hold your attention until the huge castle-style building shakes your curiosity and fears. As the van whips through the maze of upstate prison security, you look through the van bars and smoked windows and say to the driver, "Excuse me, officer, where are we?"

◇ ◇ ◇ ◇ ◇

Another added cost of your decision to choose prison life is the loss of privacy. You can no longer think in peace and quiet. You lose all rights to use the bathroom alone. It's a community setting in most cases, where anyone who walks by can see you sitting on the toilet, brushing your teeth, wiping your butt, or whatever you can imagine in performing your personal functions.

Even personal conversations during visitations with your loved ones are no longer private. If you don't want your lips to be read by someone watching the surveillance camera, you have to put down "the Gambino"—the mobster's move of placing your hand over your upper lip and mouth when you speak. This does not *guarantee* privacy, but you engage in it to make yourself feel secure when you have something important to share with your loved ones.

Every part of your life is on display in the prison experience. Just the simple things of being able to touch, hug, and kiss, or to assist someone who needs medical attention is forbidden. If your home boy, home girl, or a prison staff member falls and needs assistance, your natural human compassion is forbidden. You are not allowed to help them. Helping someone in need is viewed as you being responsible for their injury or mishap. The prison experience is so insensitive that you may not realize your heart has turned cold.

Blame is often placed on you because it's convenient. If food for dining hall meals runs short, it's commonly assumed that prisoners stole the food before it was prepared. The logic of the food service staff miscounting the expected number of meals may not be considered.

Yes, not only are you in "the experience," you are also the scapegoat of the experience.

Yet another aspect of the experience is that your sex life will be your hand, lotion, and Vaseline. Your ideal mate may be a picture in a magazine, or maybe memories of your street date or a TV star. Unless you prefer your own gender. If that's the case, you may choose to be the driver or the fender (a.k.a. "the pitcher or the catcher").

In prison, the common laws of nature work against you. Family members pass away and you *cannot* properly grieve your loss. Communicating news of a relative passing is often done inconsiderately unless you call home to receive the word directly. You may be called into the office of your Counselor, Unit Manager, Caseworker, or Chaplain for consultation or you're simply told to call home.

◇◇◇◇◇

There have been several incidents of my immediate family members passing during my decades of incarceration. Fortunately, my remaining family members understood the importance of immediately driving up to the facility to inform me in person.

I will be forever grateful to my daughter Erica Iris, my niece, and my brother Johnnie Earl (R.I.P) for driving over two hours to share important family news with me in October 1998.

A close family member dying was one of my major fears when I entered prison in 1984. I was terrified that they would die before my release.

Being in my early 20s and sentenced to serve natural life in prison was frightening. Sadly enough, I was forced to face another primary fear that October day.

At a mid-Michigan prison in Carson City, I was aware that my mother had been in the hospital for several weeks after she beckoned my sister Beverly in the middle of the night, signaling that she could not breathe. My mother and sister were the only ones living in the home our family had purchased over 50 years ago. My sister immediately called Emergency Medical Services (EMS) and my mother was admitted into Henry Ford Hospital on West Grand Blvd., in Detroit, Michigan.

Ford Hospital is where my father died, in a private room in 1983. I was the last one to visit my dad before the doctor received approval from my mother to shut off the life support system keeping him alive after 81 years on this earth. Reflecting back, it was a time in my life that I felt angry, betrayed, hopeless, and useless all at once. I didn't find out until months later that my mother had ordered the life support system shut off after my visit.

My father was my best friend, although he was 58 years old when his 32-year-old wife gave birth to me. I had never experienced the loss of a parent or other immediate family member. Mixed emotions raced through me, and my ability to cope with my father's death was not supported by groups similar to those available today.

◇◇◇◇◇

Being in the prison experience, unable to be at my mother's bedside and learning of her emergency arrival at Ford Hospital at 3:00 a.m., brought memories of my father's death. These thoughts motivated me to frequently call home in hopes of staying abreast of my mom's condition. Early on in my prison time I had permission from my mother to phone home every Sunday at 7:00 p.m. She assigned me a schedule that her limited income could afford so she could have peace of mind that I was not hospitalized or worse. Mothers worry about you when you're in "the experience." So don't ever believe that you're doing time on your own. No matter what your relations may have been with your parents, most times they can't help but feel empathy, guilt, or some sort of responsibility for the choices you make. So keep that in mind about the prison experience should you choose to pursue a lifestyle that will surely lead you to a penal institution.

Fast street cash, drinking, guns, drugs, and irresponsible behavior are all roads that lead to the experience.

◇◇◇◇◇

After my mom was released from the hospital for complications of congestive heart failure, she made the two-hour trip up to visit me. It was the strangest visit I have ever received during my incarceration. She was accompanied by my brother Johnnie and my sister Beverly. They were at the vending machines purchasing items for us to snack on when my mother, seated next to me, began explaining her final wishes and expected plans.

I sat in a daze at first, then snapped out of it and shouted, "Don't be talking like that. You aren't going anywhere."

My mother was informing me that the family house was to be left to my sister, who was instructed to send me a certain amount of money every month from the property our family had acquired since my incarceration. She told me what she expected of me in my treatment of others, and shared that all the years she spent helping strangers was in hope that someone would do some good for me if she passed away before I was released. She never wanted to go back to Ford Hospital, where my dad had passed. She spent thirty years paying for our family home and wanted to die in her own bed and not some strange hospital bed.

I realized in that moment that facing one of my primary fears of the prison experience was a possibility. Did I want to believe it or face it? No!

Frustration and confusion dominated my mind after my mother's visit. Leaving the visiting area, I felt I couldn't violate the unwritten prison code of not displaying weakness. Showing vulnerability (tears) may encourage another prisoner to seize the opportunity to take advantage of the moment as word reaches the prison yard. There are no secrets in prison. But within, I struggled with the conflict of my compassionate upbringing and the prison culture.

I reasoned in that moment that sharing a compassionate human emotion (crying) was not a viable option. Let's be clear: to show sympathy is considered taboo in "the experience." So all the things that normally come naturally to you in society are discouraged in the prison culture. Prison has rules that exist only in the experience.

◇◇◇◇◇

A week after my mom's visit my brother Johnnie, daughter Erica, and my niece arrived for a visit. Excited and grateful to see all three of my closest relatives, I entered the visiting room in anticipation. Johnnie "Barrel" had just been home off a three-year sentence for receiving and concealing stolen property. I figured he was prepared to really feel my pain and understood the value of family in the prison experience. That's why, I thought at the time, he had taken it upon himself to bring Erica and my niece to visit me since I hadn't seen either of them in over three years. Going through so much stress in everyday prison life, you long for a little happiness or comfort from a family visit.

In the excitement of seeing them, I jokingly asked, "Who died?" as I hugged them in the designated area of the prison visiting room.

You are allowed to embrace your visitors only in front of the officer's desk before and after a contact visit. You can't greet or say goodbye with an embrace or kiss in any area other than directly in front of the officer's view in most correctional facilities that allow contact visits. That is just another aspect of privacy loss in "the experience."

Erica, Johnnie, and my niece just smiled as I hugged each of them. With my arms around Erica and Johnnie's shoulders, we sat in the seats assigned by the visiting room officer.

◇◇◇◇◇

I was seated across from Erica, with a small wood grain two-by-four-foot eating table between us. After an hour or so of chatting and them bringing me up to speed on neighborhood events, I jokingly asked again, "No, for real, who died?"

I asked the question in jest. It hadn't seriously occurred to me that they would provide an answer. I was surprised by their arrival and appreciated them coming to visit. But . . . .

In a silent moment, Johnnie and my niece looked over at Erica and her "Adam's apple" moved like a jackhammer up and down her throat.

"Grandma died," she softly spoke.

"Your grandmother died?" in awe I questioned, implying her mother's mother, LaGloria.

"No, Grandma Hudson, your mother," Erica replied.

"No! Not Momma!" I blurted, as my heart began to pound.

◇◇◇◇◇

It had been less than a week since I'd seen my mother alive. She silently passed away in her own bed in her home of 30 years, paid for by my father's hard-earned wages. She didn't bother to call out to my sister in the middle of the night as she had done before.

God called her home and I believe now she is teaching the angels how to love. (R.I.P., my dear Mother Rosie. There's no other who can take the place of my dear mother.)

◇◇◇◇◇

Me? I was left face to face with my deepest fear. I wondered, what would I do in prison without Momma? It was a thought that I had never seriously pondered. No plan, no escape route, no love, no support. It was just me in this emotional tragedy of the prison experience.

The news of my mother's death made the mystic prison code of no consequence to me. I could not see anyone else in the room of 40 other family members and prisoners. It was a defining moment for me.

A son losing his mother with no ability to do anything to soothe the grieving process made me realize what was real. I always knew the importance of family support. What I didn't know was, what do you do when the foundation of your family is gone?

Just between us, the street game never prepares you for that. No tough-man, gun-toting, male egos when your mother passes away while in prison. At that time you ask The Creator to carry you.

◇◇◇◇◇

This aspect of the prison experience has no script available. So let me extend much regret to all my shooter gang stars ("gangstaz"). Karma is a bitch!

You hear about other guys' or girls' mothers passing while they're doing time, but nothing can prepare you when it's yours. The helplessness, frustration, and anger you feel are unbearable.

These and other thoughts scurry through your mind: "What will I do without my mother? She always had my back when no one else did. I could count on her when all else failed me. If I had never gotten into trouble, I would be there for my family. Why couldn't anyone save her this time? I wish I wasn't locked up. God, how could you? Why God, why me?

The unspoken words you wish you had said, the times lost, the moments not shared. The absence, the regrets, the frustration, the remorse, the "what ifs"—are all part of that experience beyond your reach. I ask you, young street thugs, "Do you still need to feel what I'm feeling?"

◇◇◇◇◇

Achieving a sense of finality over the death of an immediate family member is nearly impossible while in prison. You can't imagine the pain, mental anguish, and suffering wrong choices offer. The inability to attend the family hour. No funeral or traditional closure. The opportunity to grieve may never come. Healing is a distant process which may never be obtained. It's just you in a cold prison cell.

Once you learn of the loss of a loved one, you're left to suffer in silence in your cell. Some prisons offer Chaplain consultation, but most are not adequate for comforting your emotions.

In spite of it all, the days go on. You are forced to develop a mental defense mode of being your own mother and father, if you're able. If not, the prison healthcare will provide you with mind-altering medications, leaving you in a Zombie-like state of existence.

In the reality of prison culture, weakness is not recommended. You must keep your game face on regardless. It's not natural, but talking your pain out with just anyone is dangerous. In most cases, it's not an option!

Death is always just around the corner. So ask yourself, is this what you want for your life through the pursuits of robbery, murder, carjacking, street riches, or rims?

Your comments and questions are welcomed at Davidkhudson.com; personal emails: dkh777@live.com, or open an account at JPay.com c/o David K. Hudson #179401 Michigan and share direct.

THE THIRD TAP OF DEATH

TIME IN PRISON PRESENTS MULTIPLE OPPORTUNITIES for you to endure the death of a relative. My two brothers passed away within years of my mother's passing. My brother Johnnie, just 13 months and 13 days older than I, died in 2004 at age 46 from congestive heart failure; never seen that coming. At the time I was housed a half hour away from Detroit. I am grateful for Erica and Neice driving up to prison to break that news to me.

In 2011, while I was awaiting distribution of my first book, *Gangsta Rap for the Youth*, my oldest brother, Gregory, passed away from congestive heart failure as well, at age 59. I was not prepared for his death, either.

I learned of his passing through my Assistant Resident Unit Manager (ARUM) after my godmother, Lucille, called the facility and asked the ARUM to pass a message on to me. I was two-and-a-half hours away from Detroit, in Coldwater, Michigan.

Erica was unable to make the drive to tell me of my oldest brother's death at this time. Her driver's responsibility fees and traffic tickets for the state of Michigan, totaling $2000, were overdue. As a result, her driver's license was suspended. Like many other inner city family members, she had difficulty maintaining a valid license. In the prison experience, it is a mandatory document for visiting your loved one. So factor this into "the experience" and take notice how time changes from one family member's death to another. Your relatives' values change as do their availability and the opportunity to make you a continuous priority as the years of your prison sentence multiply. What was once important to them is now secondary, if a consideration at all.

Does it click in your head yet? You are slowly being forgotten!

Yeah, gang-star-thugs, trap starz, or hottest body babes! Out of sight, out of mind . . . .

◇◇◇◇◇

After my mother and brother Johnnie died, experiencing the death of another close relative, Gregory, truly made me think of my own mortality. When I received the sad news of my oldest brother's death, I wondered, "What legacy would I leave my children?"

"I have no material possessions—other than what fits in a footlocker and duffel bag. No expensive cars, no fine jewelry, no clothes with names I can barely pronounce, no house, no stocks, no bonds, no bank accounts. No friends that I can truly say have my back."

At this point I asked, "What will the dash between my birth date and death date represent? What truly will that dash say about the character and person I am?" Will *you* die known only as a criminal, murderer, car thief, drug dealer, gang banger, child abuser, bully, robber, rapist, or assailant? What will your dash represent? (1994-2014, sunrise-sunset).

I pondered this thought as I sat at my prison cell desk and composed a few lyrics for Gregory's obituary. I had to find ways to bring closure to all the deaths I've endured while in prison other than having someone mail me pictures of my mother and brothers in their casket ("flip top box"). [Check www.davidkhudson for more phrases.]

Experiencing the loss of your loved ones is the collateral consequence of incarceration that no one speaks about. It is the mental anguish that a person in prison or on parole may not share.

A scrapbook of obituaries to remind you of all the relatives, fallen soldiers, and friends who have passed away during the months, years, and decades of "the prison experience" is part of the street game that goes untold.

Reviewing what I knew of my brother's life—his role as the father of four children and grandfather of two children—gave me inspiration to submit a writing for his final program. The experience leaves you with few options. So Erica volunteered to read this poem to the more than 100 relatives who attended—some of whom I haven't seen or heard from in over 30 years. Desiring to be a part of my oldest brother Gregory's final rites and have my presence felt, I transcribed these words:

Am I My Brother's Keeper?

It's going on without you, that seems the hardest part.
But you can truly love now, you have a brand new heart.
All of Heaven may be present, in your Soul's view.
We had less communication between us
than Momma expected us to.
So tell Dad I love him, give our mom a kiss.
Let Johnnie know, it's the years without ya'll—I truly miss.

Ask Big Sister Gayle if she looks over the brother she never knew.
She passed away before I arrived; I believe it was the flu.
Beverly will grieve as most troubled souls often do.
Bianca, Pteris, Sabien, and Syndi, have
no father to see 'em through.

Erica has one less uncle to assist her along the way.
But TaNylah will have a caring nurse, or
maybe a "Dr. Mom" some day.
Endia and Madison are the granddaughters
who love you—oh, so much.
Rev. Jerrold McCullough is the friend who never did lose touch.

I'll continue to work hard to correct all my wrongs.
Oh yeah, I wrote my first book that teaches—more than rap songs.
Gangsta Rap for the Youth is my book's title.
Writing positive essays keeps me from being idle.

I didn't get the chance to tell you I train
rescued dogs for adoption too.
It takes love and patience when you see what they've been through.

Some people never understood your apparent selfish ways.
I know your attitude is the result of the
way we were paternally raised.
It's the "Price Persona" or the "Hudson Mystique."
Being humble and caring is not something to seek.
It's in the heart and develops as we endure.
Selflessness can't be taught, it comes as we mature.
Your first wife may have a story, your baby momma may gripe too.
But your second wife needed you in Heaven: that we never knew.
I'll let everyone know your debts are all paid.
If they should ask, I'll tell 'em, Greg's spirit will never fade.

You're at rest now, precious one; your
life in eternity has just begun.
I can't believe this dreaded day now has finally come.
Life no longer will be the same.
Your sons and I will always maintain the Hudson name.

Am I my brother's keeper?
That's a question you need not ask.
My big brother is the one who taught me.
You're never gone: only your body—not your spirit—has passed.

Rest in Peace "Big G"
Much Love, Lil Brother, David Keith

YOU ARE THE FATHER!

"A Black child born today has less of a chance of being raised by both parents than a Black child born during slavery." [1]

MOST YOUNG MALES FEEL THEY MUST have several young women in order to be a man. Through their many sexual encounters they often become fathers to children—creating several baby mothers along the way. Without a sense of truly caring for anyone, they shy away from the mother and child primarily because they lack the ability to provide for their material needs.

This is irresponsible behavior which goes along with crime and criminal thinking. Not all criminals are in jail or prison. Many will do just enough to remain with one foot on a banana peel and the other on the prison doorstep. At any given time back child support payments, failure to pay traffic tickets, or a domestic assault could result in a jail term. Slipping on that banana peel lands you in prison.

Fathering children with two or more young girls out of wedlock places you at a high risk for domestic violence or inability to pay child support. This type of relationship causes tension between you and the children's mother because it's contrary to the image a young girl may have in determining what a responsible father should be. You continue to run the street and hustle while the baby's mother is home caring for your child. She is young and

---

1 Michelle Alexander, author of *The New Jim Crow: Mass Incarceration in the Age of Color-blindness*, quoted by Nick Chiles, in "Saving Our Sons: The War Within," *Ebony Magazine*, June 2013, p.125

feels cheated of her ability to enjoy teenage activities. So frustration builds, words are exchanged, and physical confrontations happen.

It falls on the young lady to know the type of young man she is lying down with. If the young lady grew up without a father in her life, she may subconsciously seek a male to provide the fatherly love she never had.

Watching her mother's behavior in the home can also play a part in the type of young man a young lady chooses to sleep with. That still does not excuse the young man from being responsible for the child he helped bring into this world.

Committing crime to support your child is counterproductive to your goals. When you get busted, you are no longer available for your child or its mother. Serving time in prison with a child at home makes you a child abuser.

Yes, leaving your child to grow up without a father or mother in their life on a daily basis is child abuse. It may not be in the sense that you have imagined, such as causing bruises, scratches, and welts, but having a parent in prison is an injury to the child's well-being.

◇◇◇◇◇

I spent a great deal of my time in prison providing for my young daughter, Erica. She was three years old when I was sentenced to prison for the rest of my natural life. I had never been in prison before, never had any prior conviction or arrest.

In prison I sold hobby craft, worked various prison jobs, and made sure I sent my daughter a monthly allowance. If I made $30 as a porter cleaning toilets, she received a monthly check of $15. You see, my daughter never allowed me to use prison as an excuse not to be her father.

When she turned ten years old, she had her annual birthday party as her maternal grandmother always made sure of. I would phone ahead and know when the party was to take place, and make an effort to call as she blew out the candles. On this particular birthday, I sent a card containing $20, to be opened at her party along with the rest of her gifts. There were approximately 15 to 20 young children attending this party, and when she was opening my gift one young girl asked, "Where is your father? He is always giving you nice things but I have never seen him."

"Her daddy is in jail!" Erica's cousin shouted.

"In jail? Ooo!" the young girl retorted.

Erica promptly ran away from the party goers, abandoning her gift-opening ceremony by storming up the stairs with tears streaming down her face. Her voice whimpered with sorrow. Her beautiful pink and white dress with the ruffle lace around the bottom was crushed as she tripped running up the stairs in shame and guilt. Slamming her bedroom door, she refused her grandmother's commands to come back downstairs and complete the gift opening.

It was a heart-wrenching experience for me and alerted me to just how much children suffer when a parent is in prison. I realized then that I was a child abuser by the choices I made earlier in my life, with a young daughter depending on me to be a father present in her life every day. That day I realized that my conviction was not the only crime I was guilty of.

I had come to believe that I was a great father and took pride in doing all I could for my daughter from prison. It never occurred to me that it takes more than just providing for your child to make you Dad. You must be there with your child daily, whether you can provide for them materially or not. It is the everyday moments of time spent reading, watching TV, explaining how different things work, helping your child walk, talk, and understand what it takes to be safe, teaching them their home address and phone number, walking with them to the park or store. Just simple everyday things are what make you Dad.

Growing up, I looked at myself as the man my father was, always working and providing for the household. As I mentioned, my dad was 58 years old when I was born. When I was growing up, some people thought he was my grandfather. I was the last of five children. My sister Gayle passed away just after my birth, so I grew up in a household of four, three boys and one girl.

When things became overwhelming and the factory assembly check wasn't enough to cover the family bills, my father took on a second job unloading trains after he had completed his eight-hour shift at Ford Motor Company. He never scolded us about much and everything that we wanted to do was left up to my mother to decide. I wasn't taught that it is the everyday interaction with a child that makes you Dad. My father was there to provide the material means (food, clothes, shelter, transportation, bikes, toys, etc.) and occasional quality time, but emotionally, we were basically on our own. That is the model of a father I imitated supporting my daughter from prison—a provider.

My prison counselors assured me that it was a very good thing I was doing, sending my daughter an allowance every month out my prison wages. I honestly believed that by financially supporting my daughter, I was the model father in spite of my circumstances. Receiving the prison administrators' confirmation gave me the comfort that I was a good dad and doing more than most fathers did in the free world. I never realized that my constant absence was an abuse to my daughter and possibly affected the way she chose the men she had relationships with and the children that eventually resulted.

She often wondered why I was not there for her and why I had committed a crime. If I was so smart, then I should have known better than to sacrifice my role as her father and my life for my own selfish choices.

These are the thoughts your child may have and the questions surrounding her or his thoughts are ones you'd better prepare yourself to answer honestly while you're committing crimes and throwing rocks at prison fences. You are setting yourself up to become a child abuser.

Yes, criminal parents are child abusers. When I made the selfish choice to commit a crime and get sentenced to prison, I set the course to mentally abuse my daughter for the rest of her life.

It is an injury I continue to try and heal each time we talk. In various situations, I'm faced with the results of my abuse. Such statements as "When you coming home?" "Why is everybody else getting out but they won't let you out?" "When is the next time you see the parole board?" "Are they going to keep you until the dead come back alive?" "It makes me sad that my father may die state property," embarrass me when they come from my daughter.

During her college creative writing English course, she was asked to write a paper on any topic of her choice. Erica conveyed to me that her mind was somewhere else but her pen ended up writing this essay:

Incarcerated Daddy

My daddy worked as a welder at Ford Motor Company. Being an autoworker was his dream as for most young men who resided in the Motor City during that time.

After being laid off from Ford's in 1979, he and my mom had their first and only child in September of 1980. Three years later he was incarcerated.

I admire the father he is. Considering he has been locked up my whole life and a majority of his.

I was three years old when my father was sentenced to life. What exactly happened to cause this mess remains a mystery to me. I hear so many different stories about the whole ordeal. As a child I was always afraid to hear the truth. Terrified someone would tell me he was convicted of murder. How would I feel having a murderer for a daddy?

So for years I chose to be ignorant to the fact that my daddy was never coming home. Not really understanding what it meant to have life in prison, I anticipated his arrival every day. Despite what my maternal grandparents would say after they had too many drinks, I still looked forward to my daddy being on the other side of the door. After all, he did say he wouldn't tell anyone when he was getting out.

I began giving him my own personal deadlines. Maybe when I graduate from junior high . . . No dad. Okay, he'll be at my high school graduation . . . Still no dad. As an adult, I began to understand the term "Life" meant never.

Being behind bars hasn't stopped my father from being a dad at all. He is an excellent provider. When it's left up to him I don't go without anything. From mailing state checks to making sure one of his friends dropped money and gifts by, if I requested it or needed it, he made sure I had it.

I was often ashamed that my daddy was in prison. So as an adolescent I would tell people my daddy lived in California. Kids are cruel. They would never understand how I spoke so highly about my dad and had so many things to show for on his behalf, but he was never seen.

I remember at one of my birthday parties my cousin told all my guests my daddy was in jail. I ran in the house crying, knowing my best-kept secret had been revealed. Now all the questions were coming. What did he do? When is he coming home? Where does he get money from? Hell, I couldn't answer any of those questions, besides, I wanted to know the answers myself. My most frequently asked question was "What did he do?"

Well, what did my dad do? In a short version, let's just say he was at the wrong place at the wrong time. My dad was high off Valium, marijuana, and some sort of liquor. He and my mom had just got into a huge argument about leaving her car empty with no gas and she had to work the next day. My mom stormed out the house and took me with her. My dad walked to the store to get a bottle of wine.

While standing outside the store he ran into a neighborhood buddy. The guy allegedly asked my daddy a few questions and they ended up going in another part of the city to get a gun. What exactly happened in the hours after that I don't know, but there are several different stories going around. I heard my dad accepted a ride.

By taking the ride and selling a gun my dad became an aider and abettor to murder. The victim's life was over and my dad's life was thrown away in his twenties.

They tell me back in the day, an aider and abettor receives the same amount of time as the person who actually committed the crime. I know there's missing pieces to the puzzle. The only person who can fill them in for me is my dad. That won't happen anytime soon. Considering he is still "State Property."

My dad and I can talk about anything, but not what happened that cold night in 1984. My mom has offered some newspaper articles she saved. I know she offered them out of spite, hoping I'll love my dad less. That will never happen.

Today, he been locked up almost 26 years and hasn't missed a step of fatherhood. From meeting boyfriends to being a granddad. We fall out and get pissed at each other just like every other father-daughter relationship. He's pissed at me now because I haven't been to visit in over a year. It was kind of hard with my daughter turning three. Taking her to visit replays my childhood all over again.

My dad is trying harder than ever to get out of prison. He has obtained a very strong passion for parenthood due to him being absent in my daily life. He seems to forget he is already a great father to me. In the end the decision of freedom is left up to the Governor and Parole Board. Who are they to say my dad is not ready for freedom? Who am I to say that he is? If I were the victim's daughter, would I want him free? After all, he did help but it wasn't to save a life."

By Erica Iris-Denise

◇◇◇◇◇

Erica read this to her entire class. Her professor admired her courage to write on such a personal topic. Her classmates wondered if it was difficult.

As for myself, after 30 years, the injury of my abuse to my daughter is still apparent. It was something I never considered in the fast lane of street life. No one ever told me this about crime.

Child abuse is a crime. The saddest part about this type of child abuse is that it's a continuing process that may affect generation after generation. Over the years, I've seen fathers and sons in prison on separate convictions, years apart. The law in the state of Michigan prohibits relatives from being housed in the same facility. So the cycle of child abuse continues. You are in prison, your son or daughter may be in prison, and you aren't allowed to visit each other. With the written permission of the prison administrators, you can write letters to each other from time to time. Just know your every word is censored and possibly recorded.

◊ ◊ ◊ ◊ ◊

Often, when a prison sentence is imminent, a person may rush to become a parent if they do not have a child. Watching your newborn grow up through a prison visiting room is no way to be an influential parent. With just a two-year sentence you can miss some of the most formative years of childhood. And according to some state laws, you lose your parental rights when you are sentenced to two or more years in prison.

If the child's mother brings them to prison to visit, you may have the heartbreaking experience of watching your newborn cry and struggle to get back into their mother's arms when she tries to pass them to you. Your child doesn't even know you and may never really know you through a prison visit.

You can't share the special moments of watching your girlfriend give birth; your child taking their first step; the joy of feeding them with a spoon; shopping for their first baby outfits or bedding furniture; even changing their soiled diapers or cleaning a spill.

Choosing to be a thug or gangsta has voided those options for you. The goal of providing for your child or family at the most critical stages of their development is unattainable.

As the months and years pass, watching your child grow up from prison and having them ask, "Why are you in jail, Daddy? Did you do something bad? Did Mommy put you here? When are you coming home, Mommy? Can you go home with us? Why is that man in the police shirt watching us? Come on, Daddy, we about to go home." All these questions from your child on a prison visit will be the sobering reality of crime and street hustling.

These are questions you must be prepared to answer when you're out in the street, selling drugs, shooting guns to solve disputes, robbing, carjacking, gang banging, or rolling homeless people or snatching purses "to provide for you and your family." When you claim to do these things to support your family, your diligent effort condemns you. Stop lying to yourself!

Being housed in a prison cell will defeat all you profess to accomplish in your criminal state of mind. It's like digging a hole to bury your treasures while placing the dirt back in the hole you're attempting to dig. Or getting your car repaired at the collision shop and driving it out without the service door being opened. Flipping your big eight-fee re-copping just to dump the "four O's and a baby" down the manhole outside the place of purchase (see Glossary). Know

Fathers and Children

A Pew Research Center analysis of government data, "A Tale of Two Fathers: More Are Active, but More Are Absent" (June 15, 2011, Pew Social & Demographic Trends Project), found that more than one in four fathers (27%) with kids 18 or younger live away from at least one of their children. That number is more than double the share of fathers who lived apart from their kids in 1960 according to a *Lansing State Journal* article by Hope Yen (June 16, 2011).

The Pew report highlights the changing roles of parents as U.S. marriage rates and the percentage of traditional family households fall to historic lows. Nearly half of American dads under 45 have at least one kid born out of wedlock. And the share of fathers living apart from children is more than double what it was not so long ago. Among families of married fathers, children are said to be getting more attention from both parents at home than ever before. For example, college-educated men who tend to marry and get better jobs are more involved that this is self-defeating criminal behavior!

Claiming to commit crimes because you need to support your girl, guy, children, mother, father, or family is nonsense! In prison you can't support or hold down any of the people you claim to love. So how will you justify that?

Don't get it twisted. Crime has no long term-benefits. Oh, it may seem to have its gratifying moments. But I bet at least 20,000 men and women in the Michigan Penal System alone will beg to differ.

A large portion of the two million incarcerated people in this country understand the pit-fall of criminal activities and perceived rewards it offers. We know the great prison expansion of the 80s and 90s was not for us. We were already committed to the modern day slave trade. The newer facilities were built for you—our youth, whom we dads, moms, aunts, uncles, brothers, and cousin have failed. It is our obligation to share our experiences and pass "this game" down to you, so

with their children than lesser-skilled men struggling to get by.

Married fathers who live with their children are devoting more time helping their wives with caregiving at home, a task once seen almost exclusively as a woman's duty. Such fathers on average now spend about 6.5 hours a week on child care, which includes playing, helping kids with homework, and taking them to activities. That's up from 2.6 hours in the 1960s. The 6.5 hours is still just half the amount of time mothers spend per week. Still, it is a gap that is narrowing; in the 1960s fathers put in one-fourth the time that mothers did.

The Pew study also found sharp differences based on race and education. Black and Hispanic fathers were much more likely to have children out of wedlock—72% and 59%, respectively, compared to 37% for white men. Among fathers with at least a bachelor's degree, only 13% had children outside marriage, compared to 51% of those with high school diplomas and 65% of those who didn't finish high school.

you can avoid the massive incarceration rates that flood our society today.

As a courier, I am here to HELP prevent you from being the permanent underclass—in reference to the biblical cast system of the haves and the have-nots.

So let's get rich with knowledge together to avoid the perpetual cycle of incarceration. Stop selling your soul for the illusive "quick dollar" and strive for long-term prosperity by making a commitment to your community.

Remember, crime is the result of a breakdown in the relationship between you and your community.

Age, too, was a factor. Three-fourths of fathers who were 20 to 24 had children out of wedlock, compared to 36% for fathers 35 to 44. In all, about 46% of fathers ages 15 to 44 say at least one of their children was born outside of marriage. That figure tracks closely with government data showing the share of babies born to unwed mothers jumping eightfold, from 5% in 1960 to 41% in 2008.

The Pew study noted that fathers who live away from their children are not always absent from their kids' lives. More than 20% of such dads said they saw their children several times a week, and even more, 41%, kept in touch regularly through phone calls and email.

WHERE'S THE VILLAGE?

In an African proverb, we were taught "It takes a village to raise a child." This was basically believed and lived out in the 50s, 60s, and somewhat in the 70s. If you, as a child, did something in the neighborhood that you had no business doing and the neighbor saw you, that neighbor would take you home to your parent(s) and tell them exactly what you were doing. If that neighbor did not discipline you on the spot, then your parents did after they were told what you had done in the streets. Your aunt and uncles had a personal interest in your well-being as a child growing up during this era. Not to mention your grandmothers and grandfathers.

But the belief in someone else sharing the responsibility of raising you as a child and complaining to your parent took a different course in the late 1970s.

◇◇◇◇◇

Providers and Caretakers

In the Filipino culture, the first-born son and daughter are held in high regard, according to tradition, as the secondary provider and caretaker next to the father and mother. As a result, the eldest brother is automatically given the title of "Kuta," which translates to "Provider," and the eldest sister is given the title of "Ate," which translates to "Caretaker."

"Kuta" (pronounced "coo-yah") and "Ate" (pronounced "ah-teh") are titles which carry honor and respect in the typical Filipino family. Each child thereafter falls into the hierarchy, in that only the oldest boy or oldest girl is assigned the title and henceforth is responsible for fulfilling the duties instilled, taught, and honorably required if anything should happen to either parent. The younger siblings are expected to dutifully abide by tradition and show their respect by *always* calling their eldest brother or sister *only* by their title and never by their first name, even after the passing of the parents.

This honorable tradition has been passed down through many generations and is commonly practiced by Filipino families. It exemplifies a respect rooted in tradition and, most of all, love based on loyalty and trust for one another.

As young people, you have the ability and knowledge to re-adopt the honor and traditions taught generations before you. If you do not possess the skills of parenthood, lacking a father or mother figure in your life, study your history in this area and discover what helped make your existence possible.

The African and Filipino family traditions are still being practiced, and are still relevant in society today. With the high rate of generational incarceration, you need to be the one to stop the genocide of our culture. According to Bruce Western, a Harvard sociologist, and Becky Pettit, a University of Washington sociologist, 54% of inmates are parents with minor children, among them more than 120,000 mothers and 1.1 million fathers.

One in every 28 children has a parent incarcerated, up from one in 125 just 25 years ago. Two-thirds of these children's parents were incarcerated for nonviolent offenses.

Rucker C. Johnson, of the Goldman School of Public Policy, found that children whose fathers have been incarcerated are significantly more likely than their peers to be expelled or suspended from school (23% compared to 4%). He also found that family income, averaged over the years a father is incarcerated, is 22% lower than family income the year before his incarceration. Even in the year after the father is released, family income remains 15% lower than it was the year before incarceration. Both education and parental income are strong indicators of a child's future ability to make money and get a good job.

The Joys of an Incarcerated Dad

I was so proud when Erica decided to pursue a career in the medical field. Throughout my incarceration, I made it a point to continue asking her *what were her long-term goals in life.* Even though she had several jobs in various retail outlets, we often had conversations about her passions and what were the burning desires in her heart. Whether young males fathering children think about this or not, I came to understand that as men we are assigned to develop and protect our children and propel them to fulfill their God-given purpose. So when my daughter Erica graduated from the Nursing Program at Oakland University (a Pinning Ceremony),

I was overjoyed. Remember, being assigned to fatherhood your duty is perpetual.

A Gangsta's Warning

Dear Erica,

I just really wanted to take the time to let you know how very proud of you I am. You have made tremendous accomplishments in your steps toward your career goals. I just want you to know I acknowledge your determination and will to succeed.

What I find truly amazing is your tenacity to achieve your short-term goals in spite of the obstacles you face. More importantly, when you were confronted with the dilemma of having to repeat one of your classes in pursuit of your Nursing Certification you accepted the challenge, learned the lesson, and overcame temporary setbacks. Not to mention the emotional stress, mental anguish, homelessness, court battles, single motherhood, and financial challenges you endured at the time. You did not allow any of that to detour you from your goal. I found that to be extremely determinative in your ability to remain focused and know what you want in life. Those are qualities that make Champions. You are to be commended for possessing and exercising those character traits when necessary.

I admire your fortitude to stay the course and do what is required to meet and achieve the desired results of your pursuits. You should not take your accomplishments for granted but utilize them as a stepping stone to set higher goals with the confidence and self-esteem that's appropriate to take you where you have the potential to be—at the top of your career.

By all means, celebrate yourself and marvel in the goodness of God's favor. But remember that this is not the time to be comfortable and bask in the glory of your milestone success. The journey of your race is not complete and you still have the vision to manifest whatever your heart desires. Now is the time to look around you and make the choice of what type of people you associate with. I have learned that if you ever want to know what type of person you are, just look at what type of friends you have. That will tell anyone exactly who you are. This is regardless of who you try to portray yourself to be. Don't hesitate to disassociate and raise your standards of associates as you begin to climb the ladder of professional success. Being an achiever in life not only consists of a meaningful occupation but also of your human resources and the people you call friends. It's the entire picture of your life that you must begin to examine and make the decision of who supports your goals and who isn't.

You have too much invested in yourself not to be selective of the people you associate with. I made that fatal mistake and it's been three decades and I still have not been able to recover from it completely. So I'm sharing this as a precautionary measure as well as a little paternal advice. You are more valuable than what you know yourself to be. No one ever told me that, so I'm sharing it with you because I see what you may not. Examine your company!

I love you and appreciate you giving me the opportunity to share in your career success. It means a lot to me to know that you have made strides in the medical field. It is in your maternal DNA (skip a generation or two) to be in the place you are today. Just continue to take your skills and knowledge to higher levels and raise the bar on yourself as well as for your daughter. You have a lot to be thankful for in spite of your upbringing and the obstacles you had to endure. That just shows that you are made of a rare breed and nothing can stand in your way once you have made your mind up to achieve or obtain.

I just pray that you never forget just how strong you are as a woman and mother. You are doing a wonderful job in dual roles and it's not because you were privileged or had perfect parents to follow. It just seems to be a natural progression for you and it's something you need to acknowledge about yourself. Honestly speaking, I recognize! You're destined for greater things! I'm grateful to have you as my daughter and honored to be called Daddy. It's your time!

Love,
Dad

January 15, 2013

Erica Roby, L.P.N and David Hudson

Disconnected Youths

According to a study by the Measure of America, a project of the New York-based Social Science Research Council, Metro Detroit has one of the worst rates of disconnected youths in the nation. In 2012, the national report shows 17% of youths ages 16-24 are not in school or working.

Authors Sarah Burd-Sharps and Kristen Lewis studied the rates of youth disconnection in the 25 largest metro areas in the U.S. The Boston area ranked the best, with 9% of youths disconnected. Phoenix was the worst, with 18.8%. Detroit was third worst, just behind Miami, which had 17.1%. The national average is 14.7%- or 5.8 million kids and young adults.

The large number of disconnected youths—defined by the number who are not in school or working—can have severe implications, according to the authors. Kristen Lewis hopes that people become more aware of this group, of how large it is, and how serious the problem is.

A White House Council for Community Services report shows that disconnection, being adrift at this age, can have scarring effects that really last a lifetime. Author Sarah Burd-Sharps, of the Social Science Research Council, agrees. Disconnected youths have higher rates of public dependency, crime, and incarceration, and are more likely to repeat the cycle for the next generation.

CRIME IS A GAMBLE . . . AND I'M ALL IN

As a free citizen you may believe that you can do time if it's not more than a year or two. Maybe get in trouble ("catch a case"), go to court, and get sentenced to 1 to 15 years for possession or delivery of drugs, home invasion, car theft, assault, or some other offense you may think is minor.

What you don't know is that you can be held for the entire 15 years, the maximum time of the sentence. What's worse, you can easily come to prison and leave in a "flip top box" for a minor dispute or misunderstanding. My advice to you is: Fear what you don't know!

People of all ages come to prison every year with the possibility of making parole, yet face the chance of losing their life over a cookie, false pride, prison principles, a triangle love affair, too much homemade wine ("spud juice"), or some other insignificant matter.

◇ ◇ ◇ ◇ ◇

Having to face the Parole Board is another obstacle that can add years onto what started out as a year or two minimum sentence. There are no guaranteed releases on your first Parole Board interview. Ignorance of prison rules, getting involved with the wrong crowd—usually your neighborhood "friends," or not completing the recommended programming because you chose to play basketball or attempt to perfect your skills as a rapper are all factors that can extend your minimum sentence by months or years.

◇◇◇◇◇

Having been incarcerated for nearly three decades, I was scheduled to attend my fifth Parole Board lifer review on August 8, 2011. My mind began racing and wondering what I would say at my interview. I thought, "What am I going to tell the Parole Board about my crime? What are they going to ask me? Do they realize society is not any safer with me locked up? Will my 'face to face' interview be canceled at the last minute as the other two lifers' 'face to face' interviews have been?" After all, the three of us had completed our Parole Eligibility Report and had an updated "COMPAS ReEntry Narrative Assessment Summary" completed two months prior.

A Parole Eligibility Report or "PER" covers:

- a brief history of your active offense(s);
- your prior criminal record and institutional adjustment;
- your prison programming activities;
- substance abuse programs;
- psychological counseling;
- potential for community adjustment;
- health care history;
- financial assets;
- parole plans;
- and other considerations.

In Michigan's parole consideration process, the COMPAS is a compilation of about 100 questions that you are required to answer. The resulting score is an indication of your assessment risk probability; your strengths (e.g., age, home placement, environment, educational background); offense summary; criminogenic needs (e.g., substances abuse treatment, vocation/education scale); re-entry employment expectations; family criminality; mental health/depression; and re-entry cognitive behavioral scale scores. In these described areas a score less than 7 is good on the assessment scale of 1 to 10.

I scored 1 through 3 in all but one area of my COMPAS scores. That area was "family criminality," because Johnnie, who had passed away years earlier, had a criminal history. So I received a 6 in this area of scoring.

I pondered all these events the night before my review. I wondered why the Parole Board would want to see me when my Petition for Commutation was denied the previous January by the Governor's office. A Commutation request generally can only be made once every two years unless it's filed for a different reason. I was being called to the board less than seven months after my last denial. All these thoughts raced through my head in the early morning hours. I wondered if my representative and mentor—the Chance For Life (CFL) President Tom Adams—would drive two and a half hours that morning to be at my interview. He would have to leave Detroit by 6:30 a.m. to be at the Lakeland Correctional Facility in Coldwater, Michigan in time for the 9:00 a.m. hearing. I could not reason why Mr. Adams, a black millionaire businessman, would do something like that for me. I had been a member of CFL for over three years. He knew other incarcerated people who had been "Core Trainers" for 15 years. I had been surprised that he asked to be present at my Parole Board hearing when I mentioned its scheduling 28 days prior—during his monthly visit to the Lakeland Correctional Facility. It was all too overwhelming to continue thinking about. I decided to utilize the practiced prisoner stress mechanisms of minimizing and ignoring.

To avoid anger and frustration, you either minimize or ignore whatever causes you stress. Over the previous years, I had learned to perfect this technique of coping in prison. It helped me maintain sanity and avoid conflict.

Nonetheless, lying awake watching the night turn to day, I couldn't come to terms with my parole presentation and what I would say. It had been 15 years since I last had a "face to face" interview. The Lifer Laws in Michigan changed during my incarceration. The Parole Board was now required to look at your prison file without an interview to determine if they had interest in your case. I had had three consecutive file reviews without an interview, and wondered whether a board member would see me as a "Butter-and-egg man" (1930s gangster slang for a guy who ran things—a guy who called the shots and was in a position to make things happen for himself and the people around him). Being viewed in such a light could prove to be counterproductive for a prisoner in the eyes of the Parole Board. But that day was a huge shift compared to past parole considerations. I thought, what would all this mean by 10 a.m. when the interview was over? At 8:05 a.m. it all began to unravel.

◇◇◇◇◇

The unit corrections officer where I was housed rushed around the four-foot wall separating the open dorm living area from the officer's station with a look of alarm on her face.

She shrieked, "Mr. Hudson, the Parole Board wants you up there by 8:30 a.m. Will you be ready to go by that time?"

I nodded as I experienced a cold chill run down my arms and back.

Everyone in the open dorm area of my housing unit looked at me with surprise. You see, I had not told anyone in my unit that I was scheduled to see the Parole Board. Through the officer's verbal alert, all those within the sound of her voice now knew.

The word quickly traveled throughout the prison. Although most guys had been to the Parole Board many times, received parole, gone home, violated their parole, caught new cases, and returned to prison again and again, it was rare that a first degree lifer received a "face to face" interview in Michigan. What was more significant was that a lifer of my popularity throughout the penal system was getting a chance. It's not often a guy from Detroit gets this opportunity, so there was some suspicion that I had obtained this interview through political connections—that I had called an "inside favor" to persuade the Parole Board to grant my wish. Questions and accusations began to circulate throughout the prison. To those who believed I deserved a chance, it was a conversation piece for weeks ahead.

◊ ◊ ◊ ◊ ◊

Over the years, in my preparation for a possible "face to face" interview, I had talked to various correctional staff, college professors, and criminal justice students and discovered what might be expected of me in the parole/commutation process. It was clear that if a prisoner minimizes his crime/criminal behavior, he is not demonstrating that he takes responsibility for it. He must recognize that what he did was wrong and why it was wrong. So you must be prepared to accept full responsibility.

I adopted Albert Einstein's principle that "The consciousness that poses a problem won't be the same one that solves it."

It was clear that if I didn't recognize my behavior was wrong, there was nothing internally to prevent me from doing it again. If I demonstrated empathy, I recognized that others were victimized by my behavior, and how my behavior affected them.

If I recognized and understood the harm I caused, this could be a deterrent. Previously I was unaware of the effect of my criminal behavior, or just simply too selfish or caught up in myself to see the harm I caused to others. This was clear to me through my preparations and conversations.

I was taught that all this ties into remorse, which is important in many but not all cases. If a person can express regret for his crime, whether it is for the harm caused to his victim, his family, or himself, the likelihood of his re-offending (harming again) lessens.

◊ ◊ ◊ ◊ ◊

In the parole review consideration, remorse is a major factor. Remorse implies a sense of being sorry or showing some level of regret for criminal behavior. If a person shows regret and expresses sorrow for his crime, he should not want to engage in repeated criminal activity that would cause him unwanted sorrow or regret again.

On the other hand, if a person demonstrates an inability to feel sorrow or regret for having committed an offense, then the deterrent effect would lessen. For example, if a person is pointedly not sorry for his crime and has no regrets because he feels that the victim deserved what he got, then it could be argued that this person would have a greater disposition to committing a similar crime in the future should the same factors that motivated him in the first place exist once again.

Another major factor is empathy. Empathy is a quality that determines if an offender understands the total extent of harm that he has caused to a victim or in many cases to society itself. Without some measure of empathy the inmate is not able to place himself in the victim's shoes and consequently will have less understanding of the harm he caused, and a deterrent effect could be lessened.

The Parole Board also considers the inmate's ability to accept responsibility. Minimization of responsibility is weighed heavily because in a sense, and to the degree of minimization observed, the prisoner is denying his involvement in the crime and subsequent harm caused by his actions.

Many people have never spoken out loud what they did that landed them in prison. It is really important that you effectively articulate what happened. Being uncomfortable with talking about the crime can be interpreted as minimization. Again, having a complete understanding of the harm caused is important in that it can deter similar behavior and therefore lessen recidivism.

◇◇◇◇◇

Although Parole Board hearings differ, it was clear to me that my ability to feel and express empathy, to show remorse without minimizing my role in the crime, was a huge gauge to the Parole Board of my mental or social attitude.

I knew I would have the opportunity, after the Parole Board members' questioning, to make a statement. I wondered what I would talk about. How I felt about the crime and victim today? What I had accomplished since going to prison? How I have prepared for my release? How I am different today? Why I would be a good community member? I reasoned that I could not say I had done enough time. Nor could I blame others for the offense, my incarceration, or the misconducts ("write ups") I had received. I would have to work to remain calm and not react angrily to the Parole Board members regardless of their behavior or questions. I was sure of these facts, in spite of all the doubts and thoughts I had that warm August morning.

◇◇◇◇◇

When I entered the Lakeland Correctional Facility Control Center for the Parole Board interview there were two other men waiting. The attire we were permitted to wear was state blue (navy) pants and shirt with an orange stripe down the sides. My prison uniform was pressed to cleaner value (professional standards), my state-issued black oxford shoes shining like mirrors reflecting the sun. I was in another battle in the fight for my release and accomplishing something meaningful in society.

I gave my prison pass and identification card to the Sergeant at the control desk, and took a seat across from the other two prisoners in the red brick circular seating area. We spoke of the hot humid weather Michigan had been experiencing the last few weeks, the state of the MDOC budget, and the possibility of more prisons closing. No one actually spoke of "the elephant in the room"—the pending parole hearing waiting 40 yards down the hall on the other side of the sliding glass doors.

The Resident Unit Manager (RUM) coordinating the hearing came through the sliding glass doors and beckoned me to follow him. I grabbed my manuscript to *Gangsta Rap for the Youth* and hustled through the glass doors.

As the RUM and I proceeded to the video conference room where the Parole Board hearing was being held, I asked, "Why did you call me first?"

He stated, "Because your representative is here."

I was totally awed by this information. It was 8:30 a.m. and I did not seriously believe that a representative for my Parole Board hearing would drive over 120 miles that early. In all my previous hearings I had never had in-room citizen support. Still, there hadn't been any confirmation from Mr. Tom Adams and I wasn't certain he even knew the date and time of my hearing. How naïve can one man fighting for his life back be?

I did not fully know the confidence, belief, loyalty, and integrity Mr. Adams had in his mission to help reformed prisoners. These lessons are taught in his Chance For Life curriculum, but watching them being lived out was something I hadn't fully experienced anyone doing. All of that was about to change.

◊ ◊ ◊ ◊ ◊

Since 1996, the face-to-face interview had been replaced by the video conference as parole procedure. Technology, safety, and the economic state of Michigan required this cost-effective change to modern day Parole Board interviews. It saved on gas and time and eliminated the possibility of unruly prisoners disrupting the interview process. This interview was different from my June 1992, November 1996, January 2002, and August 2006 parole file reviews.

◊ ◊ ◊ ◊ ◊

In this interview the RUM instructed me to sit facing a video camera, with a round table in front of me. On the table were a roll of tissue paper and a device resembling a boomerang. It looked like something from the *Star Wars* movie or a video game control.

On the 32-inch screen appeared a woman, seated in front of files in a two-and-a-half—by four-foot steel box on wheels. She seemed to be looking directly at me as I sat in one of the two chairs in front of the screen. She was typing on what I imagined was a keyboard. It was all new to me; I had been locked up for nearly three decades and never taken part in a video conference before, although I had seen quite a few on the evening news and heard a great deal about them.

I stared at the screen as though she could not see me. The RUM asked me to move to the seat closest to the wall as he exited the room.

As I looked around the room in amazement, a voice blared through the air requesting my prison identification number. Spontaneously I recited A179401 without realizing where the voice originated. At that moment I saw the Parole Board member turn to the steel box and ruffle through the files, quickly retrieving the largest folder. She stated, "Mr. David Hudson #179401."

Automatically I replied, "Yes."

The Parole Board member said, "We should get the little things out the way while we are waiting for your representative to enter the hearing."

She asked me a series of questions (date of birth, marital status, years incarcerated, etc.) that were simple to answer—validating that I in fact was #179401, scheduled for the hearing.

◇◇◇◇◇

Nearing the end of my response to the Parole Board member's preliminary questions, Mr. Adams appeared at the conference room door through the control center's citizens search area. There was a glass window about one-and-a-half feet wide where I could see his black pinstriped suit and black and gold tie on a neatly pressed white shirt.

As the Resident Unit Manager twisted the door knob near Mr. Adams' side to open the door, the joy of seeing the CFL President at 8:30 a.m. flowed through my body as chills of elation. Immediately I sprang to my feet and greeted him with a powerful handshake. In response, he asked, "How is my main man doing?"

The tension of preparing for the interview of my life was released with the comfort of Tom Adams' presence and his willingness to support me in such a critical stage in my path of reform. My fears transformed to gratitude as the hearing proceeded.

◇◇◇◇◇

"Tell me why you're here," the Parole Board member asked.

I understood that to mean to explain the details of my conviction and what role I played in the crime. Anything less than total honesty about details can prove to be fatal in a parole hearing.

When you are *unwilling* to talk about the details of your crime and the role you played in its execution, a board member views that as "minimization"; that is, that you are trying to downplay the events or failing to take responsibility for your role. That may cause an immediate parole denial because the board member who interviewed you would not give his support for release or a favorable recommendation to proceed to the second step in the Lifer Commutation process. The second phase would mean a referral for a psychological evaluation or a legislatively mandated public hearing.

A public hearing is where the Attorney General, one or two Parole Board members, and a stenographer sit at a table while you're literally on the witness stand answering questions about every aspect of your life, from birth to the moment that you sat in that witness chair. I mean *every single* part of your life, including the crimes you may never have been convicted of—juvenile to adult and all between. The stenographer records every word you say, and what the Attorney General, Board members, and people of the public say.

In my interview I made it a point to give a complete version of events. It didn't make much sense to lie after spending nearly three decades in prison. It is prison folklore that the law-abiding citizen believes if you've been in prison for more than ten years, you're guilty as charged. There was no question in my mind, when I entered that conference room, that what was required of me was to present the most sincere interview possible in support of my release.

A Board member asked, "Why should I believe that you are empathic towards the victim's family?"

Answer: Because I now fully understand how it feels to lose a loved one. I lost my mother, brother, and countless other close relatives and friends, as detailed in my book, *Gangsta Rap for the Youth.* Most of my relatives and friends passed away from health complications but I still suffered their loss—Just as the victim's relatives suffered a loss and may not be very forgiving about their manner of death. It's understood that death is death, whether it's natural causes, accidental, or homicide. We can never bring our loved ones back.

Question: Why should this Board believe you are remorseful when you have continued to appeal your conviction but never volunteered to contact the Judge to offer to pay restitution to the victim's family?

Answer: I appealed my convictions on the advice of my attorneys at the time. I understood that I had a constitutional right to appeal. It was my belief that a First Degree Life Sentence meant you died in prison. To me that is harsh for a first time offender who had never been in any trouble whatsoever. I believe that I could better prove my redemptive qualities by giving back to the community as an example for young people who may have made a mistake or were at risk to make a mistake. I believed that I could not accomplish this if I was to die in prison. Throughout my court appeals I never expected total exoneration. I request a reduction in my sentence to a set number of years.

As far as my restitution is concerned, I have continued to pay it forward. All throughout my incarceration I have made substantial charitable contributions to homeless shelters, battered women shelters, Ronald MacDonald House for Children, and various other faith-based organizations that assist those in need. My Parole Board and prison file is full of letters in acknowledgment of these contributions.

Secondly, it became obvious to me through newspaper articles and television reports that court-ordered restitution was not reaching the intended victims or their surviving relatives. This was due to "red tape" within the prosecutor's office or the court system. Although restitution was not an official court-ordered consideration when I was convicted 27 years ago, I still took it upon myself to correct my lapse in moral judgment by paying it forward, helping those in need, and volunteering to mentor youths on my own.

◇ ◇ ◇ ◇ ◇

About a month after the conference interview I received a five-year continuance in the mail. It was my fifth time, which baffled and bewildered me. I felt I gave a sincere, heart-felt account of my actions or lack thereof. Disappointed, my family utilized the Freedom of Information Act to uncover what factors the board may have considered.

Prisoners in Michigan are not allowed access to the Freedom of Information Act (FOIA) while incarcerated. Free citizens without this legal restriction may obtain the information from a Parole Board hearing by requesting it from the Department of Corrections under the FOIA.

When my family received my Parole Summary Worksheet, they discovered some interesting conclusions and opinions that increased my confusion about why I did not earn the privilege of the majority Parole Board vote. A lifer needs six out of ten votes for the Parole Board to move forward to a psychological evaluation, public hearing, and eventually a favorable recommendation to the Governor to have his/her sentence commutated to a set number of years. I did not receive one favorable vote, but below are a few edited excerpts from the interviewer's written evaluation on the Parole Board Review Summary Worksheet Report.

RE: Prisoner Hudson, David #A179401:

Program Involvement
Regarding program involvement it is our belief:

Prisoner has been involved in Chance for Life "CFL" for the past 3 years and is a mentor. His representative (Tom Adams) is the President of CFL. Petitioner has written a manuscript for CFL, Petitioner is President of The National Lifers, a Newspaper writer for a Prison Branch NAACP, on the Board of Directors of a Prison Branch NAACP, has a Paralegal Degree, made a video for the youth, established Fathers Incarcerated Needing to Be Dad "F.I.N.D." Inc., has 2 years of one-on-one therapy, helped establish the Inside Out Program in Michigan, completed Anger Management Courses, a Restorative Justice Program, Substance Abuse Phase One and Two. Petitioner has been very involved while in prison. Prisoner said he learned the most in CFL, Critical Thinking and how to make amends. Prisoner said he wrote the manuscript because he wants to leave something behind for others, even if he doesn't get out of prison. (Not used as reason for deferral.)

Relevant Information
Review of file discloses the following relevant information.

Prisoner would like to parole to Detroit, can work at the church but has skills in Computer Refurbishing and Paralegal Certification. Petitioner does have some marketable job skills. Prisoner's representative is his Mentor and President of Chance for Life. Representative/President of CFL said petitioner has been intricate part of their program. Helping to resolve any conflicts and allowing their program to be successful as well as bringing people into the program at the facilities he has been in. Prisoner has helped a lot of people make a change. They (CFL) provide a Mentorship Program for offenders on the outside. Mandatory classes, have connections with various organizations. They can help him with jobs. They will help for the rest of prisoner's life. Prisoner had a great deal of empathy and remorse which appeared very sincere. However, no interest at this time. (Not used as reason).

<u>Regarding the victim</u>
Prisoner has extreme remorse. (Not used as reason.)

<u>Institution Management</u>
The prisoner's institutional management suggests that the prisoner:
Has satisfactory block reports . . . Interacts well with staff/prisoners . . . Follows rules and direction . . . Unit officers states prisoner has good hygiene, follows the rules, has a positive attitude, and interacts well with both staff and other prisoners. (Not used as reason.)

<u>Interview—Crime</u>
Regarding the crime, it is our belief:

Prisoner accepts responsibility . . . Prisoner expresses remorse. (Not used as reason.)

◇ ◇ ◇ ◇ ◇

This is just a small sample of the Parole Board's determination process. No outside citizen really knows why the decision to grant or deny parole is reached.

Regardless of what you've done, how much you've attempted to correct your wrong, you are still subjected to what the Parole Board believes or feels about the crime and how much time you've completed or haven't completed. It makes little difference in violent cases whether you pulled the trigger or have support, potential, or talents; there are no sure releases in "the experience." You need to understand this if you believe petty crimes offer minimum prison sentences. Avoid the wrong choice of committing crime and you will avoid the prison experience. In case you don't get it, *smart* is the new gangsta![2]

NO GUARANTEES

I have witnessed the disenchanted dreams and goals of many young men who come into the penal system and discover their hidden talents. What's worse is, they may leave prison with no genuine hope or intention of pursuing their potential careers. Lack of preparation for release, lack of work and research on their field of interest, or just plain lack of determination are primary indicators of failure.

Returning to "the hood" dissuades a weak-willed youth from taking advantage of the opportunity to sincerely turn his life around. Going home gives you "the badge of honor" to brag about how you "made it through like a walk in the park," without really sharing the pain and heartache you've endured. Even if you came into a new understanding in prison, the hood mentality (in a less determined person) won't allow you to perfect it because you will be held to the standards familiar to your family and friends prior to the prison experience. Nobody wants to believe that prison changed you.

They encourage you to forget about what you've been through and return to what you were before the prison experience. Little thought is given to the fact that going back to what you were will lead you back into prison.

Nobody knows what you've been through but *you*. You have to make the choice for yourself and not be influenced by outside sources. Do the right thing for yourself, if no one else. Keep in mind, when committing crime, release from prison is not guaranteed!

---

2 (For questions or comments contact: Jpay.com c/o David K. Hudson #179401-Michigan; http://www.davidkhudson.com or email: dkh777@live.com)

BANGIN' ON THE NET

PICTURE THIS: YOU TAKE A FEW photos of you and your homies holding guns, popping bottles, blowing blunts (marijuana), or popping E pills (Ecstasy) and upload them on your social network page. You are really excited about these new photos because they validate your "street-thug" image and warn the world no one should test your gangsta. If they do, "big thangs poppin and little thangs droppin." "Your boys" will take care of 'em with the weapons you have displayed on your Net page. (www.davidkhudson.com)

The implications of all your buddies being crazy is proven by the alcohol, drugs, and looks on each of your faces. Yeah, you all are hard, knockabout, street hustlerz, just waiting for someone to disrespect you or question your thuggish ways. It sends a message to everyone that you're not to be messed with.

The social network pictures show that you are not alone. All of you roll together and will beat down or shoot anybody who thinks they want some action out of your group of fellas and girls. Even the females in the group are looking tough with their "flags" tied around their heads, wrapped around their hands, or hanging out of their pockets, with blunts or cigarettes hanging from their lipstick. Nobody better disrespect your colors (flags) or question your ability to defend your "family" (gang members) or block (neighborhood). All for one and one for all. A solid team, no one snitches on anyone, you don't cross out one another, you follow the pecking order and do whatever you have to do to get yours. It's official now that your photos are on the World Wide Web: you are "the gang" to be reckoned with—to be respected. You will defend your turf (street) with your life, if need be.

◇◇◇◇◇

Now that we have established your status as a gang member on your Net page, let's explore just what the World Wide Web entails. Let's see, worldwide is the Central Intelligence Agency (CIA), the Federal Bureau of Investigation (FBI), the Drug Enforcement Agency (DEA), the Bureau of Alcohol, Tobacco, Firearms, and Explosives (ATF), your local Sheriff Department's Internet Squad, local police, and the Gang Squad. That's just a small indication of who surfs the World Wide Web, twitter, and social network pages seeking out criminals and their activities.

The New York Police Commissioner confirmed in 2011 that a CIA Officer was working out of police headquarters there after an Associated Press investigation revealed an unusual partnership with the CIA that had blurred the line between foreign and domestic spying.

A month-long investigation by the Associated Press revealed that the New York Police Department had dispatched teams of undercover officers, known as "rakers," into minority neighborhoods as part of a human mapping program. They monitored daily life in bookstores, bars, cafés, and nightclubs. Police have also used informants, known as mosque crawlers, to monitor sermons, even when there's no evidence of wrongdoing. However, this practice stopped in April, 2014.

◇◇◇◇◇

Consider that those guns you are displaying in your Net page group photos may have been used in a murder, robbery, or other such crimes. The law enforcement agency has been looking for one or two of "your bros" and those weapons for quite some time. But up until this point they have been unable to locate them. They heard one of "your bros" in the photo may have some information or have been connected with someone who is involved with their investigation. You have no knowledge of any of this—not even a clue that something this large could have taken place.

There you are, in the photograph on the Social Net, with all your solid team of gang-staz, showing the world you are not to be messed with. You have gone from a group of homies to a gang, now under investigation by law enforcement agencies. You are officially labeled an organization.

◇ ◇ ◇ ◇ ◇

The criminal investigation widens. Now you are a target of the criminal indictment. You may not have actually participated in a crime—yet, but you're bangin' with the fellas, smoking, drinking, and flicking up for the Social Net page.

You're not considered a "bad kid" and your mother has been encouraging you to go fill out job applications at different places. One prospective employer discovers your Internet page when he is doing a background search on you. No criminal record is apparent in law enforcement files, but this social page pops up during the background search. You were one of three candidates given serious consideration for the job. But the guns, alcohol, and drugs are the deciding factor of your future. What choice will you make? (Email me @ jpay.com c/o David Hudson #179401-Michigan)

◇ ◇ ◇ ◇ ◇

Thug-thrilled photographs can lead to far more than you can imagine when you pose for the camera. These are the challenges you face every day as a youth in the world of technology and instant messaging. You cannot afford to take *anything* for granted.

Everything you do, every decision you make, has the potential to be a determining factor of your future. That requires you to make wise choices in your daily activities, including the people you associate with, the ones you call your "friends," and the people you hang out with each day. Knowing the people you be around each day is as important as making choices, setting goals, and sticking to your plans.

At all times you must be able to make the right choice for yourself and your long-term goals. It is the short-term decisions that can alter, end, or destroy your dreams, ambitions, aspirations, and goals. These are the things you must think about when you engage in your daily activities.

It is these choices that are most important when you're about to lose focus or get discouraged along the way. Trusting in your better judgment and relying on your instincts can make the difference between the right and wrong decision that may change your entire life's course.

Prisons throughout the world are filled with people of low self-esteem who ignored their moral compass and made a decision based on emotion, peer pressure, or what seemed "the right thing to do at the time." It is the lessons and laws of society that must be your guiding light to making the correct choices.

The lure of fast money in street life is not all that it is said to be. The ones benefiting from your lack of knowledge will not share the dark side of hustling, poppin' pistols, and street life with you. They prefer to keep you blinded by the bling, the false courage of fake friends having your back, and the instant gratification of living out short-term dreams, which eventually may become your worst nightmare.

I will be the first to admit that we all make mistakes in life and in our choices. I've come to understand that no one can master life. Attempting to do so may only disappoint you along the way. We can only make a valiant effort to control the process and strive to be the best person we can be through our experiences and the knowledge we gain. The important point is to seek out correct knowledge.

Living is a year-round learning process, something that never stops. Experiencing the process brings value to your existence. Therefore, you must continue to strive to be the best person you can be.

In this age of technology you must make choices that aid you in becoming a better human being. Shooting guns, underage drinking, using drugs, and other self-defeating acts you may engage in are not moments to be frozen in time on one of the social network pages on the World Wide Web.

What you feel or believe today may not be what you think and feel in a year, a month, or even a day from this moment. Some things are not meant to be preserved. Be forever mindful of the acts, photographs, and friends you choose in life. Any of them can be a determining element in your future wealth—the wealth that comes from knowing your value in the world and the value of the blessings life has given you.

As Hill Harper pointed out in *The Conversation*,

> *There is a huge difference between self-worth and net worth. Your self-worth—your potential—has nothing to do with what's in your pocket. It has to do with character, what's in your heart, how you negotiate your personal relationships, what you place value on, how kind you are.*
>
> *Net worth is just numbers, just a bunch of paper. If we confuse that with self-worth, we will find ourselves making poor choices.*

Knowing this difference and valuing your self-worth is the true economy of life.

◇ ◇ ◇ ◇ ◇

When you have access to the World Wide Web, it is wise to develop the habit of enhancing your knowledge. The Internet is a great source for supplementing your school lessons, expanding your topics of interest, and researching class projects. The tools of the digital world should be used to access, organize, and evaluate information, not to promote criminal behavior or activities.

Instead of hanging with the wrong friends, challenge your communication skills and build relationships with students or friends you can develop your mind with.

Place new emphasis on collaborative learning and the use of digital tools to produce in-depth research projects. These experiences, when sincerely explored, can be beneficial to you later on in life.

Do not limit your ability to grow. To make right choices, you must arm yourself with correct information—not with weapons like a gun or knife.

Challenge yourself on the Internet by developing a multimedia report on a current event, a topic of interest, your desired career, or related subjects. Beginning with popular people or topics that relate to teens or your culture will help you make better decisions, find solutions, and broaden your perspective.

Compile a reference list using free information-organizing web services such as Evernote and Netvibes. Use the web-based knowledge-sharing system LibGuides. There are many positive aspects of the World Wide Web that can benefit you as a young adult. Utilized properly, these ideals and tools can assist you in making the right choices with the right type of like-minded friends. As always, the power of choice is within you.

The Trouble with Our Country

There is violence because we have daily honored violence. Any half-educated man in a good suit can make his fortune by concocting a television show whose brutality is photographed in sufficiently monstrous detail. Who produces these shows, who pays to sponsor them, who is honored for acting in them? Are these people delinquent psychopaths slinking along tenement streets? No, they are the pillars of society, our honored men, our exemplars of success and social attainment. We must begin to feel the shame and contrition we have earned before we can begin to sensibly construct a peaceful society . . . .

A. Miller, an excerpt from "The Trouble with Our Country," an article written for *The New York Times*, reprinted in the *San Francisco Chronicle*, June 16, 1968, p. 2.

LOVE IS A GANGSTA

Making the right choice is important in selecting the person we enter into a relationship with. As a teen or young adult, you must understand the power of discretion in the process of choosing your friends, whom you like, date, and ultimately, give your love to.

You may wonder what love has to do with the prison experience or being a gangsta. Generally, "most everything we do is for the love of one thing or another." That was the answer given to me by my childhood friend Trisha when I asked, "Why did you dance at private parties for drug dealers and ballers?"

She had gone to school and obtained a couple degrees in separate professional fields. In spite of that, she had three children by three different street hustlers while pursuing her education.

Trisha had a son and two daughters whom she raised as a single parent. She told me she had to do what she did to provide for her three children.

Darnell, her son, was the oldest child, Amber the second, and Jasmine the youngest. Trisha gave birth to Darnell when she was 17 years old. After the birth of Jasmine, Trisha decided she did not want any more children, and had a surgical procedure to prevent further births. As the years went on and Darnell and Amber grew up and left Trisha's home, Jasmine became the sole focus of her mother's attention. This made Jasmine more and more resentful of her mother. Around the age of 13, she began arguing with Trisha about her efforts to maintain control over her manner of dress, makeup, and other womanly attributes a teenage girl may desire to display.

Growing up as the youngest child, Jasmine had felt she did not get the attention from her mother that she needed. In her youth, Jasmine remembered all the different men coming and going from their mother's bedroom, the late night drinking parties, the children being awakened in the night by the noise of laughter, a man entering her room, or their mother's late night arguments with men.

Jasmine was awakened at sunrise several days each week and instructed to get dressed for school by her brother, Darnell, or sister, Amber. Her mother would oversleep from the late hours she kept with male companions—leaving the children to fend for themselves in preparing for school. Jasmine carried this anger inside her into her young adult years while living with her mother.

With Darnell and Amber out on their own, Trisha was distressed by the possibility of being alone as she entered middle age. She made a sincere effort to build a closer relationship with Jasmine, the only child left in the house. As Trisha had done all her life, she felt giving of herself sexually or materially was a way of showing her love and receiving love from others. She decided she would do what she could to provide for Jasmine and keep her youngest daughter dependent on her in hopes of encouraging Jasmine to remain at home. Trisha was receiving permanent Social Security disability checks from an injury and mental stress during temp work as a security guard. She had prevented an attempted robbery and was promised a huge settlement check, still pending.

◇◇◇◇◇

There wasn't anything that Jasmine wanted that Trisha didn't make a way to provide. She prepared mother-and-daughter events, dinners, and shopping outings, and even went to clubs and other inappropriate teenage gatherings with Jasmine just to show that she was a "fit-cool" mother. All this time Jasmine was internally growing more and more resentful of her mother.

Despite Trisha's most sincere efforts, Jasmine was unable to overcome the belief that her mother cheated her out of her childhood and failed to protect her as a voluptuous teen. She felt that her mother always put men before her by believing them and choosing to spend time with them rather than with her. She never really accepted the method of bonding Trisha was so diligently attempting to build.

◇◇◇◇◇

On her way home from the store one afternoon, Jasmine met this guy named Korey. His skin was caramel chocolate. He had hazel brown eyes complementing his short wave barber hair cut. He was dressed in a navy blue and white striped Polo Rocawear shirt with raw black "LRG" Jeans stomping off his pearl Nike Airs. His evening shadow mustache was well groomed, with a hair line sharp enough to cut glass.

Korey's college boy smile caused Jasmine's hands to sweat, and her heart to pound, as her eyebrows rose upon his greeting her. He was nearly two years older than Jasmine and celebrating his 21st birthday at his cousin Warren's house on the northwest side of Detroit, on Whitcomb Street.

Korey was not from that side of town. He grew up in group homes and spent time in juvenile detention centers for various crimes. He never knew his real mother, although he once lived with his cousin Warren and Aunt Dynice, whose house he was visiting in celebration of his birthday. Dynice's house was nearly three blocks off Chicago Street, near the corner of Coyle Street, where Korey met Jasmine.

◇◇◇◇◇

When Korey was 13 years old, his father, Alford Grimes, was murdered in a mistaken drug house raid. Mr. Grimes, a famous radio personality in his early years, was married to another woman when Korey's mother got pregnant by him. He did not want anything to do with Korey and never publicly acknowledged him as his son.

Al often felt guilty about his son's needs and would secretly make sure that whoever was looking after Korey had money to provide for him as he grew up. But he did not want to chance a close relationship with Korey because his wife would discover that Korey was the result of an extramarital affair. Korey never really had a family that he felt was his own. He spent countless months at his Aunt Dynice's house—the closest family he knew besides the guys from the various group homes and juvenile centers where he grew up. Having a probation officer checking up on him every week, he needed someone he could trust to cover for him and give favorable reports upon request. Aunt Dynice was that trusted soul. She had a soft spot for Korey because she knew all he had been through and felt he never had a fair chance at life.

◇ ◇ ◇ ◇ ◇

Glazing upon Jasmine's golf ball-size eyes, perky face, 40-D cups, and 37-inch hips that warm June afternoon made Korey's eyes glow like night stars. In his overwhelming desire to approach Jasmine, he licked his lips in anticipation and gathered the courage he administered in his street capers as a Juvie. In the smooth voice that Hip hop's hook singer Jeremih would envy, he crooned Jasmine off her feet while walking her home. She clearly welcomed his attention, and both chatted about their likes, experiences, and turnoffs. Their conversation was mutually acceptable, honest and revealing. From that moment on, whatever they shared would be taken to heart—literally.

◇ ◇ ◇ ◇ ◇

As the months went on, Jasmine and Korey began spending all their time with each other, sharing their most treasured secrets. She continued to get money from her mother to support them. Neither had jobs or any career goals they were seriously pursuing. Their "gangsta love" affair consisted of a lot of "X pills" (Ecstasy), "kind buds" (marijuana), alcohol, sex, and sharing of imaginary desires. Occasionally Korey would strong arm a "scrub" street hustler or an ATM customer to get money. It was his effort to bring something tangible to the relationship. Trisha had complained that Jasmine wasn't going to keep spending her money on a "no good street thug." She had the lawsuit settlement coming soon and did not want Korey to benefit from the anticipated riches. Plans for mother-daughter boat cruises and shopping sprees had been discussed before Korey came along.

But Korey never truly revealed the extent of his criminal history or let anyone know of his street hustles. What Trisha didn't know was that obtaining a passport for a boat cruise would not be possible for him.

Through it all, Jasmine had grown extremely attracted to the "intelligent thug" persona Korey portrayed. She felt safe with him. The protection her mother never provided her was manifested in Korey's gangsta loving. He received much street credit from his peers who hung out at his cousin Warren's house. All the neighborhood guys looked up to Korey because he had been in trouble all of his life and continuously emerged from juvenile detention with more knowledge and stories of criminal grandiosity to share with his peers. It was more yeast than fact, but most of the guys never knew that because they had never been to prison. So the story Korey shared was his truths. In all tales he was the victor, emerging unscathed by the horrors of foster homes and juvenile bullies.

◇◇◇◇◇

One day while Jasmine and Korey were spending time at Jasmine's house, Trisha called Jasmine into the kitchen. Korey and Jasmine had been sleeping over between Jasmine's house and Aunt Dynice's house. When Jasmine came down to the kitchen from her upstairs bedroom, her mother began to question her about Korey. Trisha's blood boiled, her eyes squinted, and her fist tightened at the thought of Jasmine spending so much time with Korey but not enough time with her to do the things they had planned. In her mind, Korey was in the way.

◇◇◇◇◇

"Why are you spending so much time with that boy? He doesn't have a job or anything going for him. What do you see in him?" Trisha asked.

Jasmine screamed, "I'm doing exactly what you did when I was growing up. You spent all your time with men when I needed you to be with me. All you ever did was tell Darnell or Amber to take care of me. All I wanted was for my mother to take care of me. I didn't need my brother or sister to do what you should have been doing for me."

"I did the best that I could for you, your sister, and brother. You need to be more appreciative of the sacrifices I made for you growing up!" Trisha shouted.

"I never asked for any of the things you did for me. All I ever wanted was for you to spend time with me and do the things mothers do with their little girls. You never gave me the quality time I needed," shouted Jasmine.

"You ungrateful little wench," cried Trisha. "I did what I knew how to do at that time. No man ever helped me raise you, nor have I allowed any man to put his hands on you. I never disrespected you the way you have me with bringing Korey into this house, flopping around and screwing him all day in my house. I don't deserve that from you or him. If he was any kind of decent boy he would not come into my house and have sex with you. I just don't understand you young people today."

"I ain't no different than the way you were. You had men coming in and out every other night when we were upstairs sleeping. You even took your ex-boyfriend Leroy's side, believing him over me when I told you he came in my room when I was 13 years old and took my virginity by force. I hate you, I hate you!"

The sound of Trisha's hand smacking Jasmine's face sounded like a car backfiring throughout the house. The subsequent crash of Jasmine hitting the stove and the pots falling off the wall cause Korey to run down the stairs with lightning speed.

"What is going on down here?" Korey asked.

Lifting herself from the floor, holding her right cheek in disbelief that her mother had slapped her, Jasmine cried, "Get your stuff, we're out."

◇◇◇◇◇

Jasmine's head throbbed with pain from the fall against the stove. A lump appeared, and the sound of drums beat in her head. She couldn't think straight. She was overwhelmed with all sorts of emotions running through her body as she stuffed her clothes in a bag.

Hastening down the stairs with a few personal items, Korey in tow, Jasmine muttered, "She get on my nerves. I wish she was dead."

◇◇◇◇◇

At Aunt Dynice's house they slept in the recently remodeled basement. A storage area in a small section of the basement had been converted into a bedroom by Dynice's "common law husband," Jerry Berry. He had felt Warren was getting older and needed his own area in the house to entertain friends. With his self-taught carpenter skills, Jerry had remodeled the basement—converting it into a paneled bedroom and a tile floor entertainment area.

Warren had a fast-food job and was contributing to Dynice's household but wasn't making enough to move out on his own. So his mother made it convenient for him to remain at home while he saved up money to purchase his own furnishings for his dream apartment. Korey made himself at home in the basement bedroom when Warren worked long hours to make extra money.

To help accommodate his cousin's probation situation, Warren often slept upstairs in his quiet old bedroom when he came home between shifts. It was better for him to rest there, away from the overhead noise and disturbance of neighborhood youth gatherings in the basement.

◊ ◊ ◊ ◊ ◊

"Were you serious about wishing your mother was dead?" Korey asked Jasmine as they lay across the air mattress in the makeshift bedroom.

"She been getting on my nerves for too long," Jasmine said. "She don't need to be on the face of this earth."

Jasmine and her mom often had arguments that had never turned physical. They generally made up or just forged ahead with their evolving mother-daughter relationship. It had never reached the point of striking one another or spilling painful family secrets while others were in the home, especially the men in their lives.

This was a significant change of events

◊ ◊ ◊ ◊ ◊

Amber had been trying to phone her mother and sister for three days. She had begun to worry when Trisha did not answer her cell or home phone. Amber felt compelled to make the long drive to her mother's westside home after phoning Darnell to see if he had heard from their mother or sister. He had not.

The drive from Canton, Michigan to Detroit had become more difficult for Amber since she decided to finish her college education and work fulltime. The time commitments interfered with her ability to visit her mother as often as she had before enrolling in college, but she made it a point to keep in touch weekly by phone. The snow-covered roads this January day were no match for Amber's maternal instincts. She had to know that her mother and sister were safe.

◇◇◇◇◇

Driving up to her mother's home, Amber noticed the broken glass from the front door storm window scattered on the front porch. Her heart began to race as she cautiously approached the front door, which was slightly ajar.

Slowly pushing against the gold door handle, the broken glass crunching beneath her feet, she softly called out several times, "Mom? Jasmine? Anybody home?"

Entering the carpet area of the house she observed the black suede pants, white socks, and partially bare flesh of her mother's legs lying across the sofa in the front room. Her mother's upper body was covered with an ocean blue blanket with white trimming.

"Momma, Momma, are you all right? Momma, Momma . . . ," Amber cried tearfully.

After attempting to shake her mother several times, she frantically reached for her cell phone and dialed 911. She noticed the large pool of dried blood surrounding her mother's body and beneath her feet as she hunkered over the sofa sobbing.

"Someone help, my mother is in blood on the couch and isn't moving," screamed Amber to the 911 operator.

"Try to remain calm, ma'am, and give me your address," the operator replied, soothingly.

"7456 Whitcomb!" shouted Amber

"Okay, honey, stay on the line with me—help is on the way," replied the operator.

◇◇◇◇◇

The Detroit Police Homicide Detectives questioned Amber for two hours. She cooperated with them fully and answered all their questions to the best of her ability.

It was clear to detectives from the hospital report that Trisha had been shot three times in the chest and face with a small caliber pistol in her home. She had lain dead approximately three days from the first gunshot wound to the forehead.

◊ ◊ ◊ ◊ ◊

Amber told the detectives of her mother receiving the settlement check and depositing it directly into her bank account. Amber knew the money had arrived and of her mother's decision not to tell Jasmine because of the huge fight they had had a week or so prior to the check arriving.

She told the police where her mother transacted her bank business and how she had owned a pistol through her state-certified weapon's permit as a security guard.

The police were aware that Trisha had prevented a highly publicized attempted robbery at the savings and loan company where she was hired to work security. In the media, she was portrayed as a hero.

The one question Amber could not answer was the whereabouts of her sister. She remembered Jasmine had a new boyfriend, but she had never met him and only knew what her mother shared.

◊ ◊ ◊ ◊ ◊

The police were debating whether to put out a missing person's report or scour vacant houses and empty fields in the surrounding area for clues. The possibility of a revenge killing, or kidnap-murder plot, was the initial lead in the police investigation. They were determined to locate Jasmine to see if she could provide clues about what had happened to her mother.

◊ ◊ ◊ ◊ ◊

Jasmine received word through the neighborhood that the police were looking for her. They had sent out a dragnet of officers, utilizing their street resources to find the whereabouts of this missing girl whose mother had been brutally murdered.

In the beginning the Detroit Homicide Division and Sixth Precinct officers were concerned that Jasmine may have been a victim of a kidnap-murder plot. But deeper into the investigation, it surfaced that she had been spotted around the neighborhood at the store and other areas with her new boyfriend, Korey Grimes.

◇◇◇◇◇

The police eventually picked Jasmine up for questioning as she came out of a local night spot about a week after her mother's blanket-covered body was discovered in their home. The police shared with Jasmine the extensive criminal history of her new boyfriend.

She learned of all the crimes he had committed as a juvenile and the recent information they had on unsolved robberies Korey was implicated in. Jasmine had known him for eight months and felt used and betrayed after hearing the stories and information the police conveyed to her.

She had believed that Korey shared all his deepest secrets with her and was her soulmate. Now, she reasoned, she was just a pawn in the larger scheme of his life. She felt it was time to save herself and give the police the story they wanted.

◇◇◇◇◇

From the information Jasmine gave the police during extensive questioning, Korey was arrested. Within 36 hours of Korey's arrest, Amber and Darnell were asked to come to the Detroit Police Headquarters for briefing.

◇◇◇◇◇

It was reported that a 19-year-old girl was accused of ordering her boyfriend to kill her mother in the home all three shared on Detroit's west side. Jasmine Works and 21-year-old Korey Grimes were arraigned in the shooting death of 43-year-old Trisha Works.

It is believed that Jasmine Works tried to use her mother's ATM card between the time Trisha was killed and the discovery of her body. Jasmine Works and Korey Grimes were being charged with first-degree felony murder and using a firearm during a felony.

◇◇◇◇◇

During police questioning, Jasmine attempted to convince the detectives that she thought Korey was just going back to her mom's house to get more of his clothing and pick up a few items for her. She told them that she was still upset with her mom and didn't want to see her at the time. Under extensive police questioning, Korey told an entirely different version.

He explained how Jasmine had said she wanted her mother dead and told him if he could get her ATM card they could have money to do whatever they wanted. He broke into Trisha's house and found her asleep on the couch with a gun. They struggled, and he wrestled the gun away and shot her in self defense.

There is no defense for breaking into someone's house. Both Korey and Jasmine are equally responsible for the murder. It makes no difference that Jasmine did not pull the trigger. She told Korey she wanted her mother dead, and he carried out her wishes. In the eyes of the law, the crime could not have taken place without her participation.

Guilty as charged: Life without the Possibility of Parole.

That is what happens when the hunter gets captured by the game. Teena Marie said,

> *Be careful about the company that you keep, or you might just end up losing sleep.*
> *Paying the price that most of us will find too steep.*

So remember, the choices you make in life are never casual; they are critical and have destiny in them.

THE KEY IS IN THE LANGUAGE

THE SIMPLE THINGS YOU SAY CAN make a difference in many situations throughout your life. You must continue to educate yourself and make it a priority to learn all the necessary aspects of whatever event, field, career, or subject matter engages you.

Words have power! It did not occur to me how powerful words are until I entered the prison system and learned that it was words on a single piece of paper that held me in prison—now for nearly 30 years.

A document many incarcerated people call the "Commitment Paper" has effects similar to those of documents once used in slavery to validate servitude and ownership. "The Judgment of Sentence—Commitment to Corrections Department" is a single-page document that has the trial judge's signature on it, along with the deputy court clerk's seal, the court's findings of guilt, and your sentence (e.g., 1-5 years, 5-15 years, 10-20 years, or Life). This document's language "certifies that this is a correct and complete abstract from the original court records. The sheriff shall, without needless delay, deliver defendant to the Michigan Department of Corrections at a place designated by the department."

The simple language on this piece of paper can keep you in prison for the rest of your natural life. It all depends on your original sentence at a jury or bench trial or a guilty plea proceeding. It is not the 17-foot fences, the prison guards, or the patrols around the prison yard that keep you in prison. It is this court document called Judgment of Sentence.

If you understand that words are powerful, you know that language is the key. Negative terms such as "bitch," "whore," "my nigga," "my dawg," and other profanities are all self-defeating language, which plays a subtle role in your value system and self-esteem. Placing negative words in your daily interactions with people only generates anger, fear, doubt, and negative conditions. You may not even be aware of the conditions worsening around you because the decline is so gradual. Your entire vocabulary begins to dwindle and you lack the language skills to communicate effectively in the business and job markets of society.

Your value system begins to lack moral standards and you fall into a pattern of doing "what you have to do, to get what you want." That's where crime and the sense of not caring about others and their rights take root. The value of another person's life has little meaning to you. Pulling the trigger on a gun is done without thinking of the outcome for those whom the bullets will hit. Drivebys are just emotions without a thought of whose innocent life is wasted. You accept the titles and glamorize the lifestyle of gangsta, drug dealer, player, pimp, carjacker, robber, thief, and all the actions that destroy the moral fibers of a productive member of society.

Failing to understand that the key is in language and your words have power lessens your faith in what's possible, and thus limits you. You settle for less and your childhood goals are lost. The simple fact that the words you use daily can have such a great impact on your future is enlightening. But what's even more amazing is that it's something you have the power within you to change. You alone possess the ability to control your actions, speech, and thoughts. Your thinking is the primary cause of all your actions and speech. You can direct your thought patterns.

◇ ◇ ◇ ◇ ◇

Selfishly you think, "Only what I do as a criminal matters." So why do you blame others for your decisions or the situation you are in? When you shoot a person, carjack, rob, steal, or burglarize a building, your only concern is what you need and how you obtain it. Yet, when you get caught or someone questions what you did, you begin to point your finger at someone else or the circumstances you feel led you into crime.

All the decisions you make in life are of your own choosing. No one can make them for you. That's just the bottom line. You may allow someone or a situation to influence what you do, but the ultimate decision is your own. You need to understand that about yourself.

If you believe that your parent, friend, brother, sister, peer, or anyone is unreasonable, then you need to be aware of your reactions. You can make an already bad situation worse by anger or poor judgment. You must look deeper into your thoughts and make sure you respond in a manner to ease tension. You are totally accountable for changing your own life. This also includes the way you spend your money.

Crime is committed mainly for money or something we perceive as valuable. But think about it: just how much do we truly value money? We spend more time scheming and planning how to commit a crime than we do on deciding how we will spend the resulting treasures. If we honestly look at it, we don't have any sense of value for our money. Yet we risk our entire life and will take another person's life for it. What sense does that make?

When you rob, steal, carjack, sell drugs—whatever you do to get money, most of the time you spend it excessively on name brand clothes at the mall, on drugs, on alcohol, on eating food that harms your body; or you foolishly give it away in a dice game, at the casino, at strip clubs, or popping bottles, or to a loved one; or you buy overpriced car accessories that will only make you a target for another "broken man's dream."

You spend crime money on whatever you think will impress others and give you a false sense of self-esteem, never realizing that you have no sense of value for yourself or the money you risk your life and everyone else's to get.

Think about all the money that has passed through your hands. Then look at how much you actually have now. You think it comes easy, so you spend it twice as fast and just as easy. You rarely consider the long-term effects of your actions or have any sense of value for the people you injure or the money you get from criminal activity. What do you truly value? Why?

The next time you tell someone to keep the change, let that be a trigger in your mind that it's really time for you to make a change. A lifestyle change!

That's all that committing crime is—a lifestyle that will lead you to prison or worse: death! There are no retired criminals with pensions, disability payments, fine cars, or large estates. Even the ones who may appear to possess those luxuries are only holding them as trustees until law enforcement busts them. All the street riches you see around you are only tokens that will be forcefully cashed in when the indictment papers come down or when the dope house robbers or the killers show up.

You can look around you and see that the odds of surviving in the game, gang, or street crew are not in your favor. Even if you think it's pleasing today, it has no promise of tomorrow. And I can't see you scheming and planning all those criminal activities with no hope for a better tomorrow. We all claim to want something more for ourselves and "we must get it any way we can because it's hard out here." What does it all mean if you're not around to enjoy the fruits of your criminal labor? As I stated in *Gangsta Rap for the Youth*," a has-been is like never was." (www. davidkhudson.com; email: Jpay.com c/o David Hudson #179401, Michigan)

Now remember, "Money talks but it does not give directions." Living in the moment is not going to satisfy your innermost craving of wanting more for tomorrow. It's a matter of knowing what's real, what's lasting, and what's just an illusion. Hustling in the street with drugs, carrying guns, shooting other people, standing up for stuff that you don't even own, robbing, raping, stealing, and any other illegal acts give just momentary satisfaction. They won't solve your long-term problems or goals. Once you think you've gotten away the first time, it may not look so bright the second, third, or fourth time. It's all gonna end and it won't be like you imagined. A sad ending is just around the corner, and that's real.

If you don't believe what I'm sharing and you're into criminal activity for the paper, then keep a written account of your "earnings" and expenditures on a daily basis. Keep a column for what you bring in, and a column on what it's spent on. Count the liquor, the Chronic, the candy bars, the fast food restaurants, the gas, the clothes, the gifts, the dice games, every single penny that comes and goes. Then ask yourself, what is the true value of your goals?

Be honest with yourself if you attempt this exercise in value. I know some of these lessons won't matter to street thugs. I understand that it's difficult to have integrity in criminal activity. Just be real with yourself. In the street game, few people, if any, are going to be real with you. "Keeping it real" is just a slick phrase. Very few actually live by that code of criminal conduct these days. Don't get it twisted. The penitentiaries are not all filled with *real* thugs. Wangstaz have their place in the experience also. It's not a pretty sight!

THE THOUGHT OF CRIME

I DID NOT KNOW THAT MY CRIME was a result of the way I think. I conned myself when I entered into a crime with absolutely no idea of how deep the effects of my actions were on my family, the community, and other victims.

You may think that robbing, carrying guns, or breaking and entering affect only the person you pulled the gun on and took the items from. Or the drugs you sold to crack heads and dope fiends affects only them. The trickle-down effects of your actions never occur to you.

Pulling a gun on someone could affect their mind and the way they act toward their children, parents, sisters, brothers, or other people around them. By exposing the victim to crime, you may make them feel obliged to purchase a weapon to protect themselves; to take self defense classes; to lose faith in the justice system; or to buy more secure door locks or bars for their home. A victim who is an inexperienced gun owner may not secure it properly, and a child may find it and carelessly shoot themselves, a close friend, a sister, or brother in the home during "a show and tell" exhibit of the new weapon. All this just because you injured a person by committing a crime.

When you think of injury, you generally think of blood being spilled, or a swollen eye, busted lip, or broken jaw. You don't think of the mental damage and how a person will react to future situations or view the people they come in contact with differently. You don't consider that person's loss of trust in others or consider their feelings or rights. Learning the root of injury is an important link in learning about yourself. If you know what hurts you, then you can put yourself in the other person's shoes and know what may hurt them also. You must understand that *all* crimes create some type of injury and come with a cost.

◇◇◇◇◇

We pay for everything in this world. There is nothing free. Stealing from the retail store causes the store owners to raise prices to cover the cost of the theft. Which in turn passes the cost down to our mother, father, community, and others who shop in the store. The primary reason large chain grocery stores moved out of the inner cities was the high rate of theft.

Now families have to go to the rural areas or outer city limits to purchase basic food items that once were available at the corner supermarket. The prices in the stores in inner-city neighborhoods are so high that families can no longer afford to provide the full-course meals they once prepared.

Crime reaches out much farther than just the items, goods, or money we take from a particular person. When you cash a bad check, the store clerk may stop accepting checks in your neighborhood. That in turn causes a huge inconvenience for the working people who may have to pay with a check or need their checks cashed on payday because they have not established a bank account. As a result of crime, the working person who has limited identification and isn't known to the neighborhood store clerk is now no longer allowed to cash the check they have earned.

There are all sorts of hidden drawbacks in crime that we may never think about in the pursuit of a hustle. It is our own self-centeredness that results in criminal thinking—the kind of thinking in which we do not consider the potential results of our actions. We have little recognition of other people's rights and feelings. We feel it's all about us and what we need. If we took two minutes to think things through or thought about how we would feel if someone hustled us, or our mother, father, sister, brother, or other loved ones, we more than likely would not do it.

We often see someone in a vulnerable situation: they leave their keys in the car door, leave their engine running and keys in the ignition in a gas station, drop their wallet, or walk from an ATM machine counting money. Or perhaps a girl has drunk too much at a party and placed herself in a situation to be taken advantage of. When you see this, and your first thought is "to get" that person for whatever valuables they possess, then you are giving over your power of choice—thinking criminally rather than responsibly.

Criminal thinking does not consider the outcome of your immediate actions. You don't feel regret until you are caught or apprehended. Then you may realize the effects of your actions on the victim, your mother, father, and loved ones, while you sit behind plated glass in the county jail.

If you took the time to consider these effects before you decide to harm or injure someone else, then you would make better choices: better choices of understanding how that gun shot will affect that person you aim your "burner" at and pull the trigger. How will their mother feel knowing that her son or daughter was shot by me?

It is the deep-rooted question that we need to consider when we have thoughts of injuring someone else. We must realize that they have a family who loves them just as much as our family loves us.

Giving in to that mere moment in the heat of passion, we may feel that we are not loved. Rarely is that the reality of our situation. We don't think about it in the deeper sense until after the fact—when we are apprehended. But it is actually something that deserves our attention beforehand. That way, we don't have to live with regrets.

It has been my experience that you will not carry a gun unless you intend to use it. And even if you originally have no intention of using it, once you carry it awhile, you will seek out a reason to fire that weapon or pull it on someone so they will know: you do have a gun. After all, what's the use in carrying a gun illegally if no one knows you have it?

Guns are fake self-esteem builders. You get extra courage when you are strapped. If trouble is not in the area, then you will seek out trouble just to be able to pull out your gun or use it to test your courage. And once you can successfully pull that trigger, you reach a point where you feel that you will never get caught. No one is tougher than you.

You reason with yourself, "I'm the man . . . I'll blast anybody . . . I'd rather be judged by 12 than carried by 6 . . . ." So you think.

But you don't realize that it's all based on the gun in the small of your back, in your waistline, or under the seat or stash box of your car. Not on the genuine courage in your heart. It's false pride, which sinks with being caught with a weapon or using it.

Your courage has little to do with what's in your heart as a human being. You don't really understand all this until you are in that jail cell facing charges for carrying a concealed weapon or assault with intent to murder, attempted murder, or the ultimate sacrifice of your freedom, MURDER. Just the slightest thought of going to jail or prison FOR LIFE never crossed your mind. As you learned in my first book, *Gangsta Rap for the Youths*, it only takes one time.

All that anger and passion built up inside of you is geared toward a person or situation that may not be as serious as you make it out to be in your mind. But that gun you carry gives you the false image that it's far more than what it actually appears to be. You are just waiting for a situation to arise where you can use it. There is this urgency boiling in your gut to pull that "chopper" and prove "I am the man . . . Respect my thuggish ways!"

What you need to understand is that not everything that happens to you is an emergency. The only emergency that occurs is what you make up in your mind. The circumstance that appears to be urgent must be looked at as the time you give deeper thought to your actions or reactions—the "pause moment," so to speak!

We always have the freedom to choose our actions, but we are not free to choose the consequences of those actions. If you're into carrying guns, then you know "murkin season" (see Glossary) is official. It's year round, no breaks! A LIFE SENTENCE is your reward. If you aren't ready to throw your entire life away, control your emotions and use your ability to think things through. On the street you cannot use a weapon rationally.

When you take the time to think and gather information, you won't be too quick to react to every given situation. You will know that not everything that happens is a direct assault on your character or a disrespect to you as a person. You will know not to take everything as if it was the ultimate offense against you.

Thinking situations through will give you the practice and ability to understand that one person's problem is not always your problem. Very often, it is that person who has the problem, not you.

We cannot control what others do, but we can control how we react to it. So know where the true power lies—within you! Once you give your power away, you lose control of the situation and become a tool for others to use as they please.

You need to be in control and handle your business in the street. Why would you give someone power over how you act or react to something? Being in control means mastering your emotions, your actions, your thoughts. It does not mean being able to inflict your will on others, or telling them what to do and then becoming angry because they don't do it. You have the ability within yourself to control your thoughts, actions, anger, and frustrations. The only reason why we get upset is because something or someone does not do what we want or think they are supposed to do. It is not because we can't do what is right or best for us. Our anger comes from us expecting something or wanting to control circumstances outside of what we can do in another way ourselves.

If you look closer at most situations or people that make you angry, you will see a way to better handle the situations and how you react to them. It takes time to develop this way of thinking. Since you continuously take time to perfect your criminal thoughts, you can also control how fast you develop this new way of deeper thinking.

Take the time to question your next move by asking yourself "Who else would be affected if I reacted in a negative way? What is my desired goal or result from doing this? Who will be injured? How would I feel if someone was to do this to me? Who will benefit?"

Make the effort to think deeply before you act or react. Take your pride and ego out of the situation. Know that not everything that happens is directed at you as a person. And if by chance it is, don't give your power of choice away by reacting foolishly. Don't give the control over yourself away to someone else because of what may be perceived as an insult to your character or position. No one can value you more than you value yourself.

Be more than a situation or a circumstance. One or two moments can be the difference in deciding your entire life. So make your choices wisely and give yourself more credit. Each of us has the ability to tap into that unlimited invisible supply of restraint through our thoughts and feelings, and bring it into our experience. So choose for you, because you're the only one who can.

Think right, make sound decisions based on proper information, and avoid the prison experience. You can determine your own destiny. No one should make that choice for you, regardless of your family situation, financial circumstances, what hood you live in, what school you attend, or who you choose to associate with. With the Creator's guidance and mercy you are the master of your own destiny.

Recognize the beautiful and wonderful things around you; appreciate and praise them. For the things that aren't currently working the way you want them to work, don't waste your energy focusing on them or blaming and accusing. Focus on everything that you want so you can get more of it. Give your attention and energy to trust, love, abundance, education, and peace. There's enough for everyone. If you believe it, if you can imagine it, if you act from it, it will come to life for you. That's the power of right thinking.

THE ABILITY TO CHOOSE

Our ability to choose has been in existence since the creation of time. When Adam and Eve were in the Garden of Eden they had the ability to exercise their power of choice. God placed Adam in the Garden of Eden to take care of it. God told Adam that he could eat from the garden but not from the tree of good and evil. If Adam ate from the tree of good and evil he would surely die. (Genesis 2-3)

But Adam chose to ignore what God had instructed him to do. Instead Adam chose to do what the devil had convinced Eve to tell him to do. In choosing to defy God, both man and woman suffered the consequence of the choices they made from the beginning of time.

We can compare these choices from early creation to the Gangsta concept in theory. The battle to conquer or take by force is shown in the devil (man's carnal nature, desires) whispering in Eve's ear that everything God had told Adam was not true. The devil told Eve, if she ate from the tree of good and evil she would not die, but experience the life of luxury, joy, and glamour—the life God did not want Adam and Eve to know about. So in her "choice of chance," she ate and offered Adam a bite in the hope that what the devil told her was true. After all, she may have reasoned, what could it hurt, since God wasn't there watching to see if their eyes really would be opened by eating from the tree of good and evil. What Eve may have failed to consider is that God has given us the power to choose. The beautiful thing about choice is that it gives us the power to take it or leave it.

What Adam may not have realized is that he would be held accountable by God for his own choices. When God entered the garden in search of Adam and called him by name, Adam hid in shame. Hearing God call him, Adam realized there was no place to hide. He emerged from hiding to face God. He told God he tried to hide from him in the garden because he was ashamed of being naked and did not want God to see him. God knew immediately that Adam had disobeyed his command not to eat from the tree of good and evil because Adam's eyes had been opened; Adam had noticed that he was naked, and covered himself with leaves. God asked Adam, "Who told you that it was a bad thing to be naked?" Adam quickly told God it was the woman who gave him the fruit from the tree and told him to eat it. This may have been the first instance of the criminal blame game.

Adam tried to deny *his* power of choice by shifting the weight and blaming "the woman." He told God that Eve had given him the fruit from the tree. When God asked Eve, she attempted to give up *her* power of choice and shifted the blame by telling God "the snake" told her it was cool to eat from the tree. Since the beginning of time, when faced with the consequences of our actions, few of us are willing to accept the truth that we control our power to choose.

As in the law of aiding and abetting explained in my first book, *Gangsta Rap for the Youth*, God held each of them equally responsible for disobeying his command and punished them in like manner. The police do exactly the same thing when you and all your homeboys/girls get caught doing a crime and are being held in the detective's interrogation room. You start blaming your codefendant: "Joe gave me the gun and told me to shoot em" . . . "I only drove the car, I didn't know Keysha was going to rob that place" . . . "I didn't do anything" . . . "We were only supposed to get the money, I didn't know Carl was going to rape that girl" . . . "I only told them where to find the drugs, they killed everybody on their own" . . . "I was high" . . . and so on.

Throughout history the power of choice has resulted in the circumstances we find ourselves in. The caveman made choices when he went out to capture another caveman's wife, hunt for food, or establish a home in someone else's cave. In most instances, his choices resulted in some type of fight, encounter with huge animals, or a territory war with another caveman's family.

Turning to 20th-century Gangsta Rappers, Ice Cube (born O'Shea Jackson) grew up in the Westside of South Central Los Angeles. While in the ninth grade, Ice Cube made a choice to write his first rhyme. Encouraged by his parents to pursue an education after high school, he attended a one-year drafting course at Phoenix Institute in 1988. The following year, Ice Cube achieved great commercial success as a member of the rap group "N.W.A." One of the group's founding members, along with Andre Young, a.k.a. "Dr. Dre," and Eric Wright, a.k.a. "Eazy E" (R.I.P.), Ice Cube wrote and co-wrote most of the material for N.W.A.'s first two albums. "Boyz-n-the-Hood" was released in 1986. Ice Cube's authoritative baritone won him a legion of fans for his N.W.A. rap anthem, "Gangsta Gangsta."

In more recent choices, the need of a Texas Ranger to avenge the threat years earlier on his father's life caused a war of no weapons of mass destruction in Iraq. Ancient libraries, valuable cultural documents, oil, and an entire country and customs were disrupted or destroyed. Dictators in small oil countries were placed on trial, killed, or exiled in the 21st century, all as a result of the choices made at some point in their lives or in the history of their leadership. In most cases the results of their choices were fatal.

The prison systems are filled with wrong choices. There are more than two million people who made wrong choices in the criminal justice system throughout America. What will your choice be?

JUST A WORD

The nation has an estimated 2500 inmates who were sentenced as juveniles to life without parole. Mandatory life without parole is reserved for first degree murder, but that covers a range of crimes: premeditated killing, intentional or unintentional death during another felony (robbery, carjacking, home invasion, rape, etc.), or aiding and abetting these crimes.

Michigan spends over $10 million a year to house more juvenile lifers than all but one other state, Pennsylvania. In all, 358 Michigan inmates are serving life for crimes committed when they were ages 14 to 17. One in five has been in prison 25 years or longer.

Juveniles sentenced to life in prison without parole tend to be black males who committed their crimes in the 1980s and 1990s. At the time of their crime, 6 were only 14 years old, 44 were 15, 110 were 16, and 198 were 17.

Before 1988, Michigan law permitted only 17-year-olds to be automatically treated as adults; 15- and 16-year-olds could be waived to adult court only if a juvenile judge approved. No one younger than 15 was tried in adult court during this period.

The juvenile reform laws began to change in October 1988, continuing through 1996. The new reforms allowed 15- and 16-year-olds to be automatically waived to adult court. A judge then had two options: mandatory life in adult prison or assignment to a juvenile facility for release at no later than age 21. The number of juvenile lifers more than doubled from the previous eight years.

In 1997 additional juvenile reform laws allowed 14-year-olds to be automatically tried as adults. Prosecutors were given the authority to designate 14 - to 16-year-olds for "adult-like" proceedings in juvenile court, and to request those 13 and younger to be subject to the same proceedings. The change gave juvenile judges three options:

- Commit the minor to a juvenile facility until age 21.
- Sentence the minor as an adult to life without parole.
- Apply a "blended" sentence where the minor would go to a juvenile facility until age 21. The judge would then determine whether to order mandatory life.

A Booth Michigan investigation into the large number of juvenile lifers in the state found:

- Teens sentenced to life without parole in cases where those who did the actual killing received less time.
- Judges who regretted imposing the life sentence, but said mandatory sentencing laws tied their hands
- Former lawmakers who supported get-tough juvenile reforms now disagreeing over the need.
- The most violent years are past. Juvenile lifer cases are on the decline, just as the number of all homicides has fallen.

◇◇◇◇◇

Because of decisions made every day by police, prosecutors, judges, and other law enforcement agencies about the guilt and innocence of inner city youths, people of African descent are over-incarcerated. The Sentencing Project reported that while in 2007 there were 412 white prisoners per 100,000 white Michigan residents, there were 2262 black prisoners for every 100,000 black residents. Nationally, African-Americans make up about 13% of the general population, but 40% of the prison population.

◇◇◇◇◇

From 1984 to 2008, the number of offenders serving life terms quadrupled from 34,000 to roughly 140,000, according to a count by The Sentencing Project.

One of the fastest-growing subgroups is inmates serving life without the possibility of parole. This subgroup jumped in number from 12,453 in 1992 to 41,095 in 2008 and represents the most costly inmates to house, as older inmates require more medical care. The cost of basic housing for an inmate serving life is calculated at $30,000 per year and can easily top $1 million over the inmate's lifetime.

RENEWING YOUR MIND

THE RYAN CORRECTIONAL FACILITY IN DETROIT, Michigan is one of the few prisons in the country that were built in the inner city. When I say "in" the inner city, that's just what I mean. Most correctional facilities are in rural areas, in the northern part of the state, or in the "boondocks," as people often refer to faraway places.

It was an exciting time for me—as far as prison life goes—when I was transferred to my hometown. In 2005 Michigan had over 40 prisons throughout the state, and I had been housed in a fourth of them. The Ryan Road and Mound Correctional facilities were the only two in Detroit and they practically faced each other.[3] You could stand in the prison yard of one and see the prison yard of the other, nearly a mile across the "mountains" created to separate them. Being transferred to the Ryan Facility gave me the hope of reuniting with my daughter, whom I hadn't seen in several years. Most young people in the inner city find it difficult to maintain the proper credentials to drive on the highways for several hours to visit their parents in upstate or mid-Michigan facilities. So distance was a major factor in the strain that was placed on ties with my daughter.

In January 2005, upon arrival at the Ryan Facility, I became involved in several prisoner programs. Primarily I attended the National Lifers of America, Inc. (NLA) meetings because I was a lifer and they offered me the opportunity to be involved with

---

3 Mound Facility was shut down in January 2012.

like-minded men. The NLA National Board was located at Ryan, and over the years in my travels to other facilities I had always desired to be a member of that board. The only problem was, you had to be at the Ryan Road Facility to be a board member. So after my transfer there, I saw an opportunity to make one of my long-awaited aspirations become reality.

In 2005 I was attending a Leadership Development Class sponsored by the Tree of Love Prison Ministry, with instructor Cardinal Mbiya Chui, when the NLA National Chairman recognized my name on the sign-in sheet that was being passed around. He approached me and introduced himself as Reggie, NLA National Chairman. I recognized his name but had never met him. When you correspond with someone for several years and finally meet them, it's like you've known one another for all those years. So he and I talked and I was placed on the call-out to attend NLA Meetings.

The general elections for the NLA are held in September of each year. After several months attending meetings, I decided to run for President of the local Chapter 1009 at the Ryan Facility and see if I could take that organization to another level. One of the requirements of the National Board is that the local President has a position on the board apart from his function as Chapter President. So upon winning the election, I was appointed the Resource Director on the NLA National Board. It was my responsibility to develop and implement programs.

The NLA by-laws were plain and gave its members a roadmap of what was allowed and what programming could be held under the NLA banner. My focus was on Legislative Seminars.

The basis of most prisoner issues has always been political. Prisoners never seem to be trusting enough of one another to pool their resources and retain the services of a lobbyist to petition their concerns to elected officials. So I decided to use the old biblical maxim of Moses not being able to go to the mountain, so bringing the mountain to Moses.

I began a campaign of writing State Representatives, State Senators, and U.S. Representatives to invite them to a Legislative

Seminar. I envisioned this as a "meet and greet" town hall meeting such as politicians host in their local communities. I had a strong passion to make this a reality since Ronald Bey had told me years ago he had attempted to organize such an event. In my letter writing, I contacted the women's facility at Huron Valley because they also had an NLA Chapter.

Michelle Bazzetta, their Chapter President, informed me that a State Representative often came into their facility to talk with the women. I was shocked by this revelation because the men's facilities had not heard anything about it. So Michelle decided to share her resources with me *if* I convinced the NLA National Board to allow women a position on that board. I reviewed the by-laws and noticed that no officers were allowed on the National Board unless they resided at the Ryan Road Facility. That would make it impossible for a woman ever to serve on the board since Ryan Road was a male facility. I immediately realized that for me to fulfill my obligation to the women at the Huron Valley Women's Facility in Ypsilanti, the board would need to update its by-laws to eliminate the residential requirement.

In pursuing this goal I met very little resistance from the sitting board members. Most wondered why they hadn't considered the idea in the past. In the end we all agreed: it needed to be done.

With the assistance of the women prisoners we organized the first NLA Legislative Townhall Meeting at the Ryan Road Correctional Facility in 2007. It was a grand success and the beginning of what proved to be a major milestone for the National Lifers of America, Inc. in the Michigan Penal System. My foundation as a respected leader and organizer was further developed through this event. I received letters from all over the state of Michigan congratulating me on the event. I shared the praise with the entire NLA National Board and Chapter 1009, for it was a collective effort and we all deserved the appreciation.[4]

Shortly after the hoopla from the Legislative Seminar had subsided, I was walking the yard and Moor-El approached me.

[4] See photos at www.davidkhudson.com.

He was a highly respected "gentleman" from the "Gangster Life" and had several newspaper articles published about his "suspected" street life iniquities. He and I had spoken on various occasions regarding our mutual belief in Islam and as members of the Moorish Science Temple of America, Inc. We had not previously discussed any programming or community activities together. But this day would be quite different: it would set my life on a course for change I had never imagined.

Mr. Moor-El began to tell me about a group he and several other prisoners had started under the National Lifers of America, Inc., at the Mound Road Correctional Facility nearly ten years earlier. My involvement with NLA made me even more attentive to what he had to share. I had never heard of Chance For Life (CFL)—not even through NLA. There was nothing in the NLA paperwork that I had read mentioning any unified organization within the Lifer group. So I wondered if this was some sort of secret that was purposely being kept from me. After listening to the entire background of CFL, I came to understand that it was only at Mound Road that CFL was established within the NLA. In the development stages it became apparent that the two groups' aims and objectives were different, so CFL had to establish its own corporate structure with by-laws and a Board of Directors. As presented to me that day in June 2007, the CFL was expanding to the Ryan Road Facility and I was offered the opportunity to become a founding member at that chapter.

It was a compliment to Moor-El's salesmanship that I was convinced to sign up for this Chance For Life Program at the Ryan Road Facility. He sold the program to me as the next best thing to getting out of prison. Because all these wonderful people would be paying for my college education while in prison and when I got out, waiting to embrace me with open arms, dropping money in my pocket, and offering me a running start. It didn't matter that I was doing Life without the possibility of parole. The offense was my first, and I had aspirations of one day being forgiven and returning to society to be a productive member. What Moor-El sold me that day was the pot of gold at the end of my dream. I wondered if he had read my mind throughout the years and knew exactly what I most desired. Even if no one else knew, I knew I wasn't the person I was portrayed to be at trial. I was determined to prove that one moment in lapsed moral judgment cannot define my entire life. What about all the good I had accomplished before and after this horrible crime that changed the lives of many people in the victim's life as well as mine? I hated that person on trial and was determined to place him in the grave and never resurrect him. This Chance For Life Program Moor-El was describing to me was the very avenue I needed. If he would just stop talking and write my name and number down so I could become a member, that would ensure my acceptance. He presented it as an exclusive program that allowed only hand-picked members of his choosing. Now, as any psychologist knows, most prisoners want to feel special, elite, and exclusive. So I was all in for that selling point as well.

After a few weeks I was placed on call-out to attend the CFL introductory meeting and find out what this program was truly about. It was a fairly new program to me and I didn't understand exactly what to expect. So when Mr. Tom Adams and Ms. Jessica Taylor walked into the room filled with about 30 other guys, I was shocked. An inner city man and woman with no ties to the MDOC had entered the Michigan Prison System with a program for change. Hell no! This had got to be a trick!

Mr. Adams entered the room with the confidence of a tiger, striding as if he's one of the smooth fellas. He did not possess the usual reserved persona that people have when entering a prison or room of prisoners with no "in room" staff supervision. He came in the door and commanded the room's respect with the experience of an Army general coming to rally the soldiers for battle. "What's happening, my man?" he asked as he shook every single man's hand with the grip of a bear. Automatically you felt the homeboy love of a brother or close friend when he approached you. Dressed in a custom made suit, matching tie, alligator shoes, designer glasses, and jewelry, he clearly represented success to any inner city youth.[5]

---

5 Photos at www.davidkhudson.com

Ms. Taylor was totally business, dressed in her beige two-piece feminine business suit and high heel shoes, and with salon fresh hair. Her golden brown complexion told you she was a woman who took extra care of her skin and took pride in her timeless beauty. She had the strut of a runway model with the flair of a confident sista. Together they demanded that you acknowledge their presence and called for your undivided attention. No need to ask, I was already there.[6]

[6] Details of the Chance For Life, T.G.I.E., Legislative Seminars and The Inside Out Prison Exchange Program can be found at: http://www.davidkhudson.com; davidkhudson@716yahoo.com

A CHANCE FOR LIFE

An unexamined life is not worth living -*Socrates*

THE CHANCE FOR LIFE ORGANIZATION (CFL) is a prison-based habilitation program that provides educational, life skills, and behavioral modification curriculums to the incarcerated. The objective is to offer a progressive transformation program to individuals while they are in prison, in an effort to prepare them for a successful transition back into the community. The purpose of the CFL Organization is to increase community safety by reducing recidivism through education.

Chance for Life currently provide a comprehensive training curriculum to the general population at several facilities throughout Michigan that consists of—but is not limited to—*The Mediation Center* (where prisoners are taught certified mediation techniques and skills); *Critical Thinking Techniques*; *Communication Skills*; *Conflict Resolution Techniques*; *Parenting Education*; *Men Concerned with Youth, Family, and Friends*; *College Scholarship Program*; and the *Transformation Awards Ceremony*. The Chance For Life motto is: *Be Ye Transformed by the Renewing of Your Mind* (Romans 12:2).

That scripture is very significant to me because my mother (RIP) expressed to me that "your life path can be determined through a series of incidents or a series of choices. Or your life path can be determined by the sheer recognition that you can change it at any time." My understanding is, being transformed by the renewing of my mind helps me reconstruct my pattern of thinking. Mr. Adams told us on the first day that "I'm coming with the silver and gold you can't get from the robbing, killing, and running game. It's acquired by the renewing of your mind."

He went on to say that, "It's not about what happened to you. It's about how you feel about what happens to you." It was in that moment that I sincerely decided to make a career switch. I reasoned from my entry into prison that I didn't choose these circumstances to become worse; I wanted to use them to become better. CFL was the program for that improvement.

Ms. Taylor addressed the group and informed us that "our in-look is what determines our outlook." She stated, "I'm not here to teach you anything because you already know everything. What my job is—help you unlearn some things you been taught. I know you all have that warrior spirit in you and you always think the best way to solve conflict is with violence. But I want you to know that the only enemy you face is the 'inner me.' Once you get out of your own way, you can get out of prison and stay out. The ability to manage problems and situations determines the difference between a janitor and a CEO. I'm here today to help you be a CEO."

I asked Ms. Taylor, "When will we graduate from the curriculum that the Chance For Life Organization offers?" Her response was, "When you die." She told me that "Chance For Life is not a program, it is a way of life. Once you make the decision to transform your thinking, you will continue to grow, but I'm not preparing the blessing for you. I'm preparing you for the blessing." Ever since that day, I have been a Core Member of the Chance For Life Organization.

As a Core Member of Chance For Life, I learned that I have no choice but to change. Core Members must desire change for their sake and see this program as the only way to effect that change. Change requires refraining from what you want to do and doing what you do not want to do. You have to develop endurance. You must eliminate old ways of thinking and acting and replace them with critical thought patterns and actions.

As a youngster I didn't utilize the willingness or ability to discover the seeds of my own destruction. It was always a struggle to perceive my complicity with antisocial thinking. The admission of guilt is hard. As I mentioned in my book *Gangsta Rap for the Youth*, my family nicknamed me "Destruct-o." Back then, it was much more reassuring to see the world in terms of me hanging out with the slothful instigators of the monstrous violence that surrounded my life daily. I drifted through those periods of life like a ship on the high seas with no destination, carried along by prevailing tides flowing up and down, often tranquil and lovely in the calm. I did exactly what my social circle was doing. The priority of my decision making was, "What are my buddies into?" I matched my thinking and my values to whatever the guy I was hanging out with was doing. As long as he was doing it, it must be OK, was my standard of reasoning. I hadn't built my own set of independent values in regards to my dreams, goals, status, or the realities of my life. My probability estimating was undeveloped. I lacked the ability to make decisions before all the facts were in. It was these unexamined probabilities that were an underlying factor in my life's failures and the unexpected danger signals I never bothered to recognize.

As a Core Member, I have come to understand that I needed a head, a heart, and guts: a *head* to evaluate myself critically, to learn, and to solve conflict rationally and solve problems constructively; a *heart* to give me sensitivity to other people, empathy, and compassion; and *guts* to endure the hardships of this new way of life which oftentimes causes one to be labeled and scorned in "the experience."

Critical thinking, conflict resolution, and effective communication are important elements in the CFL Curriculum. Growing up I wasn't aware that I should analyze situations, equate my thoughts and feelings, and then determine which thoughts are risky and what would enable me to adopt new attitudes and change my antisocial behavior. I grew up never realizing that a great deal of conflict in my life was a result of my inability to communicate. As a youth I had a severe speech impediment: I stuttered uncontrollably and was unable to effectively express my thoughts and feelings. So I acted out in frustration and anger for much of my life.

When I was growing up, everything my sister, brothers, and I did was followed by the question "What will the neighbors think?" I became concerned with only what others thought and felt—totally disregarding and detaching from my own feelings, thoughts, and moral compass. After my father passed away in 1983, I was not thinking constructively. After several months of grieving, feeling sorry for myself, and blaming God, I began to exclude all the verses and instructions given to me in the Scriptures. I gave up social control, all the appropriate "shoulds" and "should nots," cultural norms or, in a sense, conscience.

I grew up accepting my family values of "What will the neighbors think?" I was afraid to think or do otherwise. My individuality was polluted by street myths and subcultural philosophies. I went with what was criminally expected that cold January 1984 night that sent me to prison for life. That is, what would be thought of me if I didn't go along with the program (crime)?

After experiencing the death of my mom and two brothers, I began to ask, "Why were my home training and values so concerned with what the neighbors thought? Growing up, why did I believe that if someone hit you, it was okay to hit them back? Why did I accept that violence was a viable solution to conflict? Why was I taught to just go along with the program? Did all my beatings with a razor strap and extension cord throughout childhood affect my life? Did the physical abuse produce feelings of violence in me? What was my genealogy like?" Why didn't I show a greater value for womanhood? During a knife attack in my youth I was held up as a human shield while screams echoed in my ear: "Don't hurt the baby, don't hurt the boy." Being swung from side to side with my little feet dangling at every swat of the blade, I held my eyes open in fear and dismay.

In re-evaluating my upbringing I came to comprehend the basis of my behavior. This was the initial process of my objective evaluation of my own personality and behavioral structure. Crippled by domestic tradition, I had little positive data about my own value, let alone the value of others. As I began to self-reflect, evaluate my family values, and transform my thinking, I came to realize that most of my childhood consisted of a critical struggle for physical and psychological survival. This struggle persisted throughout my teenage and young adult life.

It wasn't until several years in "the experience" (prison) that I focused on and made a conscious effort to get in touch with my thoughts and feelings. Redirecting my thinking, values, and belief system helped develop *my* self-worth. It motivated me to make positive contributions to life and not be influenced by negative people or a subculture.

I made progress in stages through the Moorish Science Temple of America, Inc., one-on-one psychological therapy with Dr. Charles Harper for two years, the University of Michigan (U of M)-Dearborn *Inside Out* Program, U of M-Ann Arbor PCAP, The Greyhound Inmate Experience (T.G.I.E.), various related MDOC programs, and self-help studies. My most noticeable change occurred through a combination of the teachings of Prophet Noble Drew Ali (M.S.T. of A., Inc.); the Chance For Life Curriculum; T.G.I.E.; and U of M-Dearborn *Inside Out.*

The *Inside Out* Prison Exchange Program ® promotes social change through transformative education. It is an initiative directed at deepening the conversation—and transforming ways of thinking—about crime, justice, and related social issues. Founded in 1997, and a national (now international) program since 2004, Inside Out brings college students and incarcerated individuals together as peers in a classroom setting that emphasizes dialogue, critical thinking, collaboration, and the creation of new ideas. Inside Out aims for the students' holistic engagement to create personal and communal change where "everyone serves, everyone is served." I helped found and was selected for the original Michigan *Inside Out* Program and THEORY Group in 2007 because of my academic talents, perceived intellectual curiosity, openness, genuine interest in personal growth and social engagement, and my ability to work in collaboration. This is a semi-confidential group, so my discussion of my transformation process in this group is limited.

Learning in the M.S.T. of A. that *man is born with unlimited capacity for progress* made the words my mother shared about change come to life. My attraction to Moorish Science was that it allows its members to study all spiritual leaders (Jesus, Mohammed, Confucius, Buddha). I embarked on a journey through "the experience" to be the best person I could be. In the biblical Scriptures I read that Paul and John transcribed their most profound lessons while in prison. I hadn't considered the significance of the Scriptures and the physical restraint on their authors prior to "the experience." In the religious doctrines, Prophet Daniel, Queen Esther, Zerubbabel, Jeshua, Ezra, disciples, saints, prophets, and theologians were at one point or another in "the experience." I was awed by this revelation. Coming to understand that greed rises from wrong ideas of satisfaction, anger rises from wrong ideas concerning the state of one's affairs and surroundings, and foolishness rises from the inability to judge what correct conduct is, I was determined to change my life.

In my decision to change, nothing was more decisive than the value judgments I made about myself. I knew I was more than a person who made a horrible error in moral judgment one very cold night in January 1984. My willingness to self-evaluate my life and present circumstances had a significant effect on my thinking process, feelings, past beliefs, values, needs, and goals.

I came to accept that the world doesn't owe me anything, it doesn't revolve around my needs, and I don't have a right to touch or take anyone else's belongings. I once believed that everything anyone did was a direct assault on my character and my entire existence. Not being able to properly internalize information or communicate my feelings and beliefs, I often reacted in an aggressive and negative way. Reevaluating my behavior through a very painful and objective process, I changed my beliefs and thereby changed my values system. The losses of my father, mother, and two older brothers were turning points in my evaluation process. I am no longer motivated by material possessions. I don't let what others say or think of me determine my actions. I've taken control of my life and accept responsibility for my own actions and fate. I no longer use my parents, upbringing, environment, or associates as an excuse for what happened or did not happen to me. Prior to my transformation, I was the president of the blame game club. Everything that I ever did or whatever happened to me was someone else's fault.

In the CFL Core Training I learned how to resolve conflict, listen to others, respect opinions, accept diversity, and communicate effectively without prejudice or personal bias. I have a greater appreciation for life and know that it's not within my judgment or power to determine who should live or die. My morality has been reprogrammed and I'm able to take action with moral certainty, established principles, and integrity.

Integrity is a primary character trait in the CFL Curriculum. Instead of having a moral stance, I developed a moral position. I remember from my stock boy days at Daily Discount stores in Detroit that integrity is important to success in business. I learned that it's even more critical if you want to be a person of influence. Ethical principles are not flexible once you become a Core Member of CFL. That's why it's crucial to maintain integrity by taking care of the little things. I know that character is made in the small moments of our lives. I understand that anytime I break a moral principle, I create a small crack in the foundation of my integrity.

So when times get tough, when a criminal partner or the past haunts your everyday existence, it's challenging to act with integrity. But CFL isn't for the weak-minded or fainthearted. I've come to understand through CFL that character isn't *created* in a crisis, it only comes to light. Nor do circumstances make a man; they simply reveal him to himself.

Over the years, CFL has afforded me the opportunity to mentor troubled youth—active gang members who have entered into the adult prison system and other men under 25 years old. I've acquired a great deal of knowledge and respect from these young men who feel that no one really cares about them or what they become. It has made a significant difference in the lives of several young men, who have made the decision to turn from criminal activities. They have inspired me and unlocked the door to my life's purpose through their candid participation in the Youth CFL curriculum. In the first Youth Transformation Ceremony some of the toughest gang members were speaking with tears, explaining what a significant difference the CFL program made in their life. There wasn't a dry eye in the assembly. It inspired me.

We can all make a difference if we just decide to help one young person at a time. "Each one teach one" is a solution to street crimes and violence. Society cannot change until persons change. In many cases, our youth just don't know! It is my purpose to share my experience in hope that it sparks a flame in a person that will encourage him to change his life and make a positive contribution to the world. In CFL we teach youth that treading the path of adversity will lead to the destination of their dreams. They must be willing to trust in their vision to properly succeed, with patience and perseverance. They are encouraged to discipline themselves to hold on to their perspective. For us as mentors, the challenge is growing with them and not growing apart. The miracle is in the process. We will drown in our destiny if we don't see who they are now. If we can't grow with the youths, then we can't go with them. This is a concept for redeeming our children that others must adopt. The power of our words and actions can inspire the next generation to do their best. Love has no loopholes. Society in general is telling the youth they were born to lose; CFL teaches they were built to win. We can no longer blame our history for not grabbing our destiny.

The Holy Koran of the M.S.T. of A. teaches that: *reflection is the business of man and;* that *The only devil from which man must be redeemed is self, the lower self. If man would find his devil he must look within; his name is self* (Chapter 3, Ins. 21).

The lower self is your physical desires. If you want to find the strength to make changes in your life, just look within and conquer your demon self—the thoughts you have that breed hatred, slander, lewdness, murder, theft, and everything that harms. Those thoughts and actions are rich in promises, but poor in blessedness and peace; they offer pleasure, joy, and satisfying gain, but give unrest, misery, and death.

L-R

(Bryan Crenshaw-Legislative Liason, Michigan State Senator-Martha Scott (2008), Michigan State Representative-Alma Wheeler Smith, Jessica Taylor-Chances for Life, Tom Adams-CFL President, Dorothy Leonard-A 'Daughter of Isis)

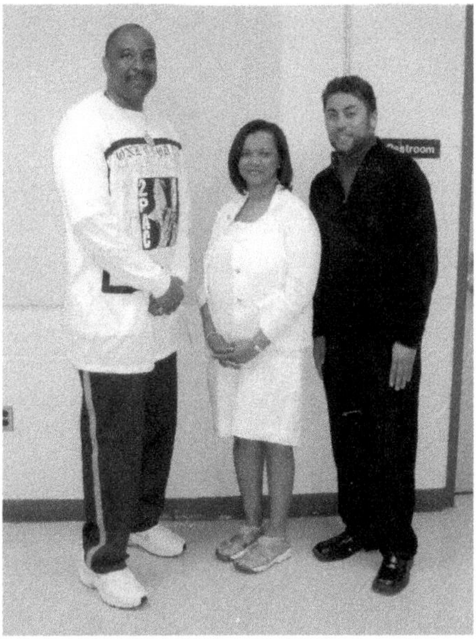

Caption:
(Detroit Council Woman Monica Conyers)

L-R

Legislative Assistant to Hansen Clark, Michigan State Representative-Alma Wheeler-Smith, Michigan State Representative Coleman A. Young II presently State Senator 2014, Ms. Felecia Tyson-Juvenile Legislation, Bryan Crenshaw-MDOC Leg. Liason, State Senator Hansen Clark US Congress(2010)

"Sweet Berry" The First T.G.I.E Greyhound David trained for Family Adoption

(Gregory Hudson (R.I.P 1952-2011)

L-R

(Brother Antoine "Tiny" Thomas Bey, Mentee Ran away from Compton, California at age 15. Caught cases in Michigan and was sentenced up to 40 years, David K. Hudson, Mentor)

Brother William Parker Bey (R.I.P 1912-2006)

L-R

Shelli Weisberg, ALCU-Michigan; Jeff Gerritt, Detroit Free Press Editorial Writer Ysabel Benejam, Juvenile Second Chance Inc. (2008)

The Honorable Michael Switalski, Michigan State Senator 10th District (2007).

Detroit Mayor Kwame M. Kilpatrick (2007)

Legislative Townhall Meeting (Ryan Correctional Facility) David Hudson Bey; State Rep. Alma Wheeler-Smith; Ms Tyson; State Rep. Paul Condino Bryan, MDOC; Legislative Assist; Mich. Senator Hansen Clark; NLA #1009, Secretary

Center Seat: Doreen Roberts Bey (Smith Bey); Brother Rasul Muhammed; Brother Victor Muhammed

Rev. Dr. Sidney C. Griffen, Sr.-Board Member of Fundamental Fairness
Professor Rahman. Ph.D.-University of Michigan-Dearbom

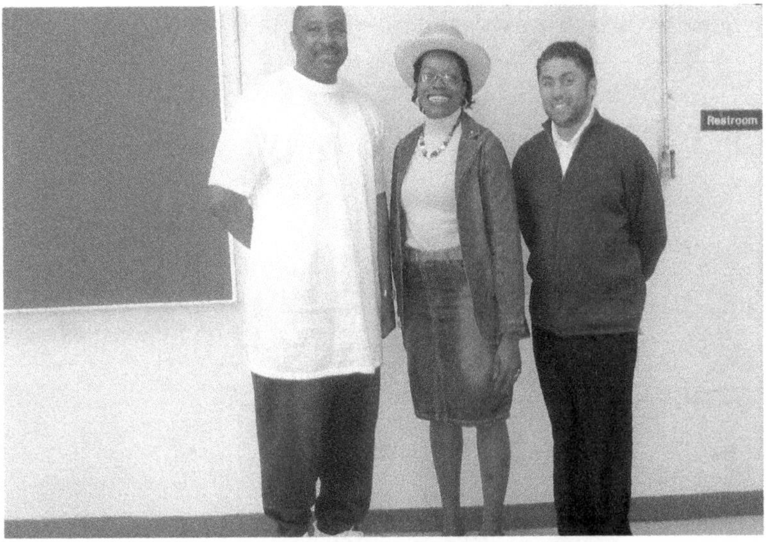

The Honorable Deborah Thomas-36th District Judge, Detroit Michigan

Mr. Lett, Legislative Aid; Mich. State Representative Shanelle Jackson; State Representative Paul Condino, State Representative Bert Johnson State Representative Alma Wheeler-Smith

Mother Audrey Ayo; Sister Ife Nabawi; Felecia Tyson; Ysabel Benejam; Detroit NAACP Members

Bryan C., MDOC; Rev. Naomi; Rosalind Worthy. Gospel for AIDS; Ayanna's Mother; Sister Ayanna (2008).

A GIFT WORTH KEEPING

(A Chance For Life Participant's Testimony)

In the spring of 2011, I was chosen to participate in the Chance For Life Program. At first I was admittedly skeptical that this program would be any different from many other programs that usually failed to meet a goal of "change" within the participants' personal lives.

I was soon proved wrong!

As the weeks of spring turned into the early days of summer, I found myself eagerly attending the weekly sessions. My eagerness was warranted by the fact that I *was* experiencing a change in my life—a dramatic change at that!

With the help of the materials presented to my classmates and me, I began to re-evaluate the ways in which I thought, how I perceived people and situations, and, more importantly, how I communicated with others.

The instructional materials were, by all accounts, rather simple, and yet when presented by the hardworking facilitators, they clarified things for me as nothing else had done. In the short span of 12 weeks, I learned more about myself (and how I interact with others) than I had ever learned in my 51 years.

Much of what I learned about myself was not pleasant, and I came to regret how I had prejudged those around me. Yet the class gave me the hope to be able to make those necessary positive changes in my critical thinking—changes which, I hope, will make me a better person. Moreover, the class gave me the inspiration to not only help myself, but to share this valuable knowledge with others so that they, too, can be better people.

The CFL Program was free, and the effort from the facilitators was truly a labor of love. It was, simply put, a gift—and it's one that I will keep with me always.

By David Ward #174359
Used with permission

THE GREYHOUND INMATE EXPERIENCE

IN 2011, WHEN WORD BEGAN TO spread throughout the Lakeland Correctional Facility that the greyhound rescue program was going to be re-implemented in the Michigan Department of Corrections, there was fervid anticipation. The program saves the lives of retired racing greys and prepares them for family adoption once their careers are deemed over. Several hundred men in the facility were excited at the thought of receiving an opportunity to apply for the rescue program.

The idea to partner prisoners with rescued canines that were retired, abandoned, or abused first entered the Michigan penal system in 2007. However, in 2009 the greyhound program was shut down due to some complications with the racing dog owners in Florida.

Through their tenacity and their undying love and dedication for the greyhound breed, Ron and Gaye-Ann Weaver found new racing owners in Alabama, and the greyhound program was re-introduced to the Michigan Penal System. In 2011, the Weavers established the nonprofit corporation T.G.I.E., *The Greyhound Inmate Experience*. Let me share a little about this caring couple.

Ron Weaver is the prototype of the strong supportive man. He is quiet and remains in the shadows of his life partner, but has the charisma to emerge and dominate the atmosphere with his charisma. When Mr. Weaver speaks, he's like E.F. Hutton: people listen.

On the other hand, Gaye-Ann exudes the fire of a bubbly motivator. She enters the room with an electrifying zeal that commands your undivided attention. Her personality awakens the joy in your soul that has been longing to surface. She exemplifies the verbal acrobatics of the most proficient orator, who can soothe your life's sorrows. She is an angel cloaked in a garb of flesh.

◇◇◇◇◇

Soon after the application and screening process was completed and the elite 20 men were selected, each was asked to work as a team to formulate a name, logo, and mission statement for the program. Collectively we gathered and decided that these should honestly reflect our views, what the program means to us, and what we feel the public should understand about the potential and rehabilitative effects of men training and developing skills in socializing retired greyhounds. It was our primary goal that the rescue program be about the canines.

So as the dogs began to enter the facility and the training and socializing process got underway, something magical started to take place. You see, it could never be just about the rescued dogs when the trainers are the ones assigned to instill discipline, respect, obedience, and social values and to teach commands (laws) to the canines. You cannot give or teach another something that you do not possess yourself. So the same principles of discipline, respect, obedience, and social values the men were assigned to instill in the dogs became a driving force in their lives also. Through the process of teaching the greys, the handlers are learning life's lessons. Just watching the evolution of trust in humans and the rejuvenation of their spirits is a self-fulfilling perk a trainer anticipates on the first day a new grey arrives.

As handlers the men experienced a rejuvenation in the program and in many cases a transformation in their lives. The feeling of belonging and having the compassion and empathy to care for another living being are just a few of the qualities they have regained. As incarcerated citizens, they receive from T.G.I.E. the opportunity to show they are capable of rising to the challenge—and of being responsible without hourly monitoring of their every move. They accept the challenge in seeing the growth and development of each canine from entry to exit in the T.G.I.E. program. Receiving this chance in and of itself gives them a sense of obligation to improve. The handlers accept the responsibility to nurture, groom, care for, train, address medical needs of, and socialize our retired greys. Not only are they giving the dogs another chance at life, but the men are also afforded another opportunity to demonstrate life's redemptive characteristics. Knowing that someone trusts them to care for a living creature raises their sense of awareness that they are still valued and people do count on them. After two successful training exchanges with ten greys per session, the program was expanded to include 40 handlers and a corporation clerk.

The Greyhound Inmate Experience is more than just a rescue dog program. It is a human restoration opportunity for any qualified incarcerated person who desires to restore his self-confidence, self-worth, and values and show his rehabilitative qualities to the world. Sure, the handlers love and care about each and every greyhound as though it were their very own newborn child. Just as important, expressing their love and care gives them pride, dignity, and confidence in knowing they can still experience the human qualities of compassion, empathy, and remorse after the damage they have caused others. The greyhound rescue program breeds the redemptive qualities spoken of in the biblical sense of man atoning for his misdeeds. The handlers are able to give back to society in their present circumstance by restoring life, liberty, and the pursuit of happiness in the neglected breed of the greyhounds. T.G.I.E. has become a phenomenal experience that words cannot adequately describe.

The reality of knowing that you have played a role in saving a life and giving another creature on this earth a second chance leaves you with a wish to never cause any more pain or discomfort to another of God's creatures. You only want to give the joy and spirit of accomplishment through teamwork that you acquired in your newfound experience of revivifying life and instructing another in the proper etiquette of a civilized society.

It is the mission of The Greyhound Inmate Experience to provide the best trained and socialized retired greyhounds for family adoption and to demonstrate what a great breed the greyhounds are. This will be accomplished through patience, skilled training team-work, and utmost compassion from the trained incarcerated handlers. It is the handlers' sincere desire to be part of the rescue process and to educate the public on the importance of the redemptive qualities and rehabilitation benefits of this program.

Yes, T.G.I.E. is a dog rescue program, but it is a human redemptive program also.

Learn more at www.tgie-greyhounds.org.

FAMILY TIES

I'd dream that I could tell Martin Luther we made it,
But half of my black brothers are still incarcerated.
Ludacris, "Do Your Time"

During the mid-80s on through the early 90s, the television program *Family Ties* was familiar to most people in our communities. But to an incarcerated father, "family ties" means much more than a half-hour television show. Although the concept of "It takes a village to raise a child" was a central theme throughout the program, family ties have a greater meaning to the incarcerated.

Having the support of family is paramount. It is often a determining factor in how well a man adjusts to incarceration—how he does his time, and it has a direct impact on the rate of recidivism. When the families of incarcerated men maintain constant contact through visitation, emessages, letters, cards, and phone calls, the stress and hardships of everyday prison life have less impact once those men are released.

Studies have shown that prisoners who had the support of their families throughout their incarceration were less likely to re-offend or return to prison on a parole or technical violation. In many instances, when faced with a crisis that may factor into extending their time in prison or committing another crime that returns them to prison, men with family ties will think of more than just themselves.

Incarceration is a time of reflection for most people. It allows you time to look back over your life and view it from the outside looking in rather than inside looking out—although literally that's the parody. During this time of incarceration you think of all the positive things you've done for your family and others.

Going through the court system and listening to the prosecution's theory exposes you to enough negativity about yourself. You feel remorseful and often regret the actions or inactions that resulted in harming others. You then seek to search your soul for the positive aspects of life and your circumstances. You wonder why family and friends have abandoned you at the most critical time of your life—when you need them most. But in many cases your family feels that you have left *them*; it was your choices and decisions that caused family ties to be severed.

Over time, without family ties to demonstrate the affirmation of unconditional love, the feeling of remorse can turn to bitterness. When the neglected individual eventually returns to society, he may act out his long-growing bitterness on his loved ones. Simply keeping in close touch and effectively communicating with an incarcerated person can help alleviate a substantial amount of recidivism and crime.

Family members must take it upon themselves to be honest with their incarcerated relatives. People have good intentions and say things they would like to do; it could be something as simple as a promise to visit or send money. But we know the road to hell is said to be paved with good intentions. For whatever reason, something else occurs that is more pressing or interferes with "the promise" made to the incarcerated person. Loved ones must be frank with prisoners. Truth is one burden that most incarcerated people sincerely welcome. It aids them in keeping in touch with what is—not with what seems to be or what family members feel they need to say.

What society may not fully understand is that prison life breeds a co-dependent behavior for those subjected to its environment. You depend on the system to tell you when to wake up, when to eat, when you can use the rest room, when to take a shower, when to go to bed, when and where you can stand or go. The small things in the day-to-day activities of a prisoner are dependent on what the system tells him to do. That co-dependent mentality is embedded in the prisoner and he comes to count on what others tells him. The systematic psychology of co-dependency, a major factor in the conditioning of the incarcerated, is often taken for granted. It spills over into the way a prisoner interacts with his family. That's why prisoners are sometimes manipulative and self-serving. (Example: *"If you don't send money, . . . you don't love me,"* or *". . . someone is going to hurt me,"* or *". . . I am going to hurt myself," etc.)* It is the prison conditioning of a co-dependent environment that breeds the basic human traits of the Maslow Hierarchy in the incarcerated. (See Glossary)

Consistent family ties help counter this systematic induced behavior. Most prisoners' drive to legally achieve is greatly diminished once they are released from prison. The first major obstacle they encounter may provoke a feeling of *the world being against them*. Never once do family members realize it's a mentality that was reinforced during their incarceration. Men are told on a daily basis, "You don't have nothing coming because you are a prisoner." Day in and day out, just to get a roll of toilet paper a man may be faced with this administrative prison maxim. It plays on a man's will to achieve when it has been imbedded: "He don't have nothing coming."

It takes the love of family to restore and maintain a man's pride while he is incarcerated. The love of family can provide the sense of worthiness that one needs to endure the negative effects of day-to-day prison operations. Family ties can never be taken for granted or minimized. They cannot necessarily be measured by financial support. A simple letter, card, or visit can mean the difference in a person's life when he's faced with administrative prison maxims and related conditions.

No, you as a family member may not have put a loved one in prison. But your family ties can surely make the difference in what type of person returns to society as a son, brother, husband, uncle, cousin, friend, or neighbor. Let's be clear: family is not just a bloodline relative. Family is the core of humanity which connects us all through divinity and matter—the spiritual and the physical aspects of mankind. If you haven't figured it out yet—yes, we are *all* in this together!

Your comments are welcomed at davidkhudson.com and e-message the author at jpay.com c/o David K. Hudson #179401 Michigan

Send Release and Commutation Letters of Support for David K. Hudson A179401 to: Office of The Governor, State of Michigan; George W. Romney Building,
111 South Capitol Ave., Lansing Michigan 48909.
www.michigan.gov

MANHOOD PLEDGE

As a man, I now lay down my garment of maleness, boyish and childish behavior, and pick up the garment of manhood, and live my life as a responsible and reliable man.

It is my solemn covenant that I shall love and respect who I am. I shall strive to protect the young, respect the elderly, and express honor and kindness to my female counterparts within the communities throughout the world at all times.

My brothers and sisters are safe from my hands, tongue, and thoughts. This day have I truly become a man in both the spiritual and physical sense. This day, and all days to follow, I shall endeavor to seek knowledge of self and the world. I shall endeavor to ingest the knowledge and transform it into a proper understanding, and thereby putting the two virtues into application, to establish my wisdom for the betterment of self and my people.

This pledge I do solemnly partake:

Signed: ______________________________

A GANGSTA RESOLUTION THE URBAN STRENGTHENING SOLUTION WE THE PEOPLE

Urban Initiative

Purpose:

We The People Urban Strengthening Program is a grassroots effort to prevent and reduce crime, unite citizens, establish effective intervention programs, and restore the responsibility of maintaining a safe urban community to the hands of The People.

Implementation:

We The People will utilize community colleges, universities, various urban nonprofits, religious communities, the business community, and community-based organizations to formulate the curriculum and maintain a weekly mentoring program for youths and returning citizens (parolees, probationers, ex-felons, children at risk, children of incarcerated parents, dropouts, etc.) in targeted communities to monitor the initial progress of this initiative—preferably high crime areas in urban and rural communities throughout the world.

The buildings of these various organizations—local school buildings during and after hours, churches, etc.—can all be used as learning centers for teaching youths and returning citizens various skills. Soliciting, uniting, and utilizing the current resources that are in the urban community will be the catalyst to spread this initiative. Classrooms may be gender-oriented.

Funding:

The Governor and Legislators and/or City Officials will set aside 10 to 40 million dollars for result-based progress to the We The People Program by providing an opportunity for non-profits and other organizations to apply for the funds through a grant program. Only 15-20% of these funds will be allowed for administrative cost. This will assist in maintaining the integrity of the We The People Initiative. An increase may be allowed as the documented results improve for any specific applicant.

Public Awareness:

A media blitz involving local television, radio, and neighborhood billboards will be implemented to notify the public of this initiative. Various everyday citizens, business owners, and city officials of different age groups and multicultural backgrounds will be recorded as stating a variety of slogans beginning with "We The People":

> We The People will not tolerate crime in our neighborhood;
> We The People are taking back our streets;
> We The People are accepting responsibility for our youths;
> We The People will no longer tolerate violence in our schools;
> We The People are the ones that matter;

The power to save our communities is in the hands of We The People, etc.

A community based-seminar will be held to inform the leaders in the targeted communities of the implementation of this program in their area and how they may apply for the grant funds. Complete details and the criteria necessary for participation in We The People will be given at the seminar. Seminars may be held over a period of time. (Flyers, posters, pamphlets, etc. will be distributed).

Programming:

The program is being implemented in a specific area with the theme of "One Youth, One Block at a Time." The People's Initiative Committee will establish training, classes, and lessons in critical thinking, conflict resolution, communication, mediation, proposal and grant writing skills, substance abuse awareness, the legal process, resume writing, peer groups, financial management, starting a small business, family planning, parenting skills, construction, computers, healthy eating, and so forth. A great many urban youths are not exposed to or taught these basic life-skills.

As a failsafe for progressing urban students, this program will offer high school seniors the opportunity to jumpstart their college education by enrolling in basic clerical, writing, and other skills at local university and community college campuses, thereby providing extra support to some who may have considered college an unrealistic goal. The program will expand their vision and instill hope for their future. The high school students will work with local mentoring college advisors in preparing them for university or community college courses when they are ready. The program is similar to the 1970s Senior Intensified Program in Detroit and the current Early College Program at Lansing Community College, in Lansing, Michigan. We believe motivating students to break away from the traditional high school setting into a program that lets them reach high and progress quickly is also helping the state and city strive for something better.

The mentoring program (five years minimum) will be required to check immediately on program participants if they are tardy or absent or have problems to discuss.

Human Resources:

Ex-felons, parolees, and probationers will be encouraged to go into targeted communities to recruit and identify youths, potential criminals, felons, dropouts, and at-risk teens and direct them to the resources that the various organizations and community leaders offer. For every youth or felon the parolee or probationer brings into the program, a portion of their restitution, parole time, or electronic device fees will be deducted from their obligation to the state. (For example: $100, a month of supervised parole, a week of electronic fees, etc.). Other incentives may be offered.

Radio personalities, local rappers, church congregations, single parents, teachers, musicians—all influential community persons will be asked to refer potential clients into the program in the targeted area. Mentoring contacts include:

100 Black Men of Greater Detroit. Web: www.100blackmendetroit.org;

Alpha Phi Alpha Esquires. (248) 756-0072;

Brothers Making A Difference. (313) 231-4899
Web: brothersmakingadifference.org

Men of Style and Substance. Email: wm@williammalcolm;

Tau Kappa Kappa Chapter. Dr. J. Marks, email: jaybmarks@yahoo.com

Empowering Males to Build Opportunities for Development and Independence (EMBODI), Delta Sigma Theta. (313) 577-1710; Web: detroitdeltas.com;

Kappa Alpha Psi. Web: detroitalumnikappa.org.

<u>Course in How to Improve Parental Control</u>:

This would be an eight-week course for parents. Faculty may include psychiatrists, probation officers, ministers, pediatricians, educators, psychologists, and an obstetrician. The subjects to be taught and discussed with parents are: Producing change in youth offenders; Understanding moral values; The Relationship between freedom and love; Problems of underachieving; Crisis prevention; Why children "play stupid"; Rescue and repair of "poor students"; Building healthy attitudes toward sex and marriage; Emotional control; and Responsibilities of parenting.

The Role of Law Enforcement:

It is the belief of the We The People campaign that law enforcement should be the last resort of failed community intervention. We propose that law enforcement be assigned to patrol and maintain order on the surrounding targeted area and give the program an opportunity to take effect. The organizations and program participants will maintain an open line of communication with law enforcement supervisory staff and keep them abreast of any potential violations in the targeted area. We The People authors believe law enforcement generally makes pleas to the public for help in solving crimes, so why not empower the citizens from the beginning to aid in the prevention and intervention of crime before it develops? Law enforcement can help organize citizens watch groups in the targeted community and hold training seminars to educate those citizens on what to do.

We believe that offering the urban community the chance to have an active role in crime prevention will be more effective than locking criminals up *after* the fact. This initiative will potentially save the state millions of dollars in incarceration costs and crime and victims rights costs, as well as relieve the tension on law enforcement and help build a better relationship with the community.

Conclusion:

By CFL-LCF Inside Core Members

It is We The People's position that crime is simply the result of a breakdown between the individual and their community. This program is the first step in restoring those broken ties.

How can the community be made safer? Neighborhood Watch Groups; Build better relationships among neighbors (put the neighbor back in hood); Use the unclaimed money from "Crime Stoppers" and "America's Most Wanted" and police drug forfeiture money to sponsor community events, skating parties, picnics, block parties, bingo games, etc.—all to build community relations.

How can we get perpetrators not to commit crimes? Educate the potential criminals/ youth at risk through criminal justice seminars where pro bono lawyers, legal aid firms, paralegals, and ex-felons teach and share the consequences of crime, the penalties of crime, and the loss of freedom. Most youths do not have a clue of the consequences they face. Enlist parolees and ex-felons to give lectures on their experiences at these community-based events as a community service requirement upon release.

SHOUT OUTS

To all mothers, fathers, sisters, daughters, brothers, sons, aunts, uncles, boyfriends, and girlfriends who have sacrificed, supported, and stuck by their incarcerated loved ones in "the experience"—To Jeff Cooper, for your copy editing—To Judge Avern Cohn: Thank you for your judicial honesty and moral support—To Professor Michael Eric Dyson, author and my Webber Middle School buddy, "the rose which grew from the concrete"—To Everett Dyson Bey—To *We the People* contributors: Marty "J.R." Richmond, Donnie Harris, Bruce Michaels, Robert England, Johnny Whitt, Jon Martin, Abdul-Kareem "K-9" Jordan; thanx for being 2real and the first to purchase my book *Gangsta Rap*, K. Smith—To all my Chance for Life Core Members: "Life in the Power Circle"—To the membership of the National Lifers of America Inc.—To Father Tim Kane, Rev. Sidney C. Griffen, Sr., Verna Hines, Tara V., J. Graham—To all (40) T.G.I.E. dog handlers—To Tone Berry-Knall—To Darnell and Carnell "twin" Bates—To Cardinal Mbiyu Chui (Rev. Moore)—To Tanya Harp-Davidson, *From Crack to Christ*—To the Brenda Cook family, the Price Families—To Adrianne D.R., find your true values within: LaShan C., take the back seat once in a while and just enjoy the ride; thanx to all "the ladies" for your encouragement and the *diced pineapples; take it to the head*—Labora L.,—"The Michigan Moors"—To "Kool-Aid" Jenkins Bey—Dwight Carveil Love (R.I.P. 2014) To Kimball Gaskins-El Sr.—Ricky Rimmer Bey—To Sheik J. Alexander Bey—To Charnell "Nuttyboy" Goodwin, Charles "Chuckie" Hurst, Sanchez Fletcher, Joshua "Jay" Donahue, for all your support in my financially challenged times while self-publishing *Gangsta Rap for the Youth*—To Romando Valeroso, thanx for your reviews; we're in the dark with our light so bright—To R. Simpson Bey: "we winning over here"—To Roberto Anselmo for your contribution to *Providers and Caretakers*—To "Family Hustle," T.I.: Young Jeezy, Gucci Mane, Scarface, Yo Gotti, and Ricky "The Boss-Rozy" Ross: "I did it for them all"—To Detroit Rappers, for all your material that gave me the inspiration—To Seven tha General—To C. Picaso, Doughboyz Cashout, Ty, SwappDawg "The Gator Man," capital city in tha house—To W.T. "Billy" Williams: "the hardest part of life is people can't play their role"—To Kennedy and *Pacific Street* Smith Families—"Lil Will" Merryweather—To Colfax & Cobb "Peanut" (Essie Brown Family)—To Elonda R—To "Bigg Boppa" Knight Bey—To Mother Lucille Steele: *God is my Guide and our Salvation*.

To Judge Greg Mathis, "the TV Judge": thank you for not forgetting where you came from, homeboy—To radio personalities John Mason, Tom Joyner, and Mr. Chase: your DJ skills have carried me through—To Tyler Perry for all the recorded plays and movies you've created for us to share laughs at through *the experience*—To Steve Harvey for giving brothers hope of their unlimited capacity for progress—To Alicia Keys, Hallie Berry, Megan Goode, Nicki Minaj, Trina, Jennifer Hudson, 106 & Park, VH1's Basketball Wives, Love and Hip hop, and all the beautiful sisters who have given men dreams and hope in *the experience*—To the haters: thanx for the motivation, "Open your eyes, I'm a blessing in disguise." F.A.M.E.,—To all "the girls" who abandon ship in this experience, thank you for leading me to *my* true love, my wife.

POETRY CORNER

Solitary Confinement

Mesmerized by the time
While slowly losing my mind:
White walls caving in
"Help", screams from the men within.
Continuously pacing this 6 by 10 room,
My head flooded with thoughts of gloom.
Haven't received a letter in months,
Dudes yell about speakers they had in trunks.
All I used to want was peace and quiet
Now I just want to scream and riot.

Nothing here but my pen and thoughts
As I think about the life I lost.
My actions got me into this,
Right now thoughts of death bring me bliss.
No more pain, suffering or consequences;
Only eternal peace as I lie deep in the trenches
No one to talk to so I write it down,
How deeply I wish I could turn my life around.
I used to want the flashy life,
Now all I dream for is a child and wife.

Twenty-six days until I'm free,
Then back to waiting to leave the penitentiary,
I always say I wouldn't come back again.
But sometime misery is my only friend,
Nothing to do but write, eat and masturbate;
Sit for the other twenty hours and silently wait.
I lay in bed trying to sleep at night,
Continuously awaken by guards flashing lights.
Sometimes I wanna pray though I don't believe,
But this voice inside says there's something greater than me.
My actions got me in so my actions will get me out.
When I make it through the hard times a man will sprout.
For now I'm a boy who's insides bleed,
With an empty heart full of need
For the love
Of my family.

Kawan D. Fields Used by Permission

I Understand

I understand this is hard for you,
Taking care of home and your man too.
Working hard and dealing with drama;
Stressful fights with Babydaddy's Babymama.
Bills piling up and junior running wild
Sometimes you feel alone a helpless child.

I understand at times you wanna break down,
Laying in bed wishing I was around.
Your love is strong, precious and unique,
In love with a prisoner, visiting every week.
You persistently go through a lot to live,
All you ask for is the same love you give.

You're doing your best to keep our love strong,
You say, "no matter the years it's never too long."
I understand you love me but need something more,
Me not being around, you could never ignore.
I can't be there to comfort you and hold your hand,
But you try to stand strong in a pit of quicksand.

I understand everyone says you're crazy for waiting,
You should live your life and get back to dating.
In my heart I know you deserve better,
But I can only express my love in every letter.

At times my absence really starts to show,
How much more you can take;
You really don't know.
You deal with this void everyday, faithfully.
That's why I cherish you more everyday, gratefully.
But if you ever need someone to hold your hand,
Just know I appreciate your love
And... I Understand.

Kawan D. Fields Used by Permission

Sister I Apologize

To the woman of the earth
Which brings forth birth;
To the love of my life,
My mother, my daughter, my wife:
There are no excuses
Why the blood of Kings have become useless.
"I vow to stand strong
And hold down home
As soon as I finish this time
The world will be mine."
Just a couple of lies you're fed
Waiting faithfully in an empty bed.

Bills needs to be paid
And children to be raised,
The one with you
And the one that's caged
Single mothers holding down the throne
Say, "I can do bad all on my own!"
As man, we should be,
Taking care of our family.
I got a Cadillac, three baby mama's
And a flat screen in my room at my mama's
My oldest say he wanna be just like me,
Getting money in these streets.

You stay by my side,
When drama comes - you down to ride.
Late nights you cooking dinner
While I'm in the streets.
Quick money make me feel like a winner
While you alone in the sheets.

Kawan D. Fields Used by Permission

When we go out I can't open yo' doe'.
I'm busy checking out that otha hoe.
Six years down
And you still around!
Say you remain faithful
And for that I'm grateful.

Little man need shoes
But I got the poker blues
You say, "Jr. comes before the rest."
I say, "I need a blood test!"
I call the shots cause I'm the man,
Disagree and feel the power of my hand.
I've fed you lies throughout time
And even through late night cries you remain mine.
Now you say you've had enough
But I call your bluff
I get a letter a week later
With a picture of you and this white man, in gaters
You say you're tired of Black men,
The good ones either gay or six feet in
I act hard but I lose the disguise
I was tough but alone I'm the one who cries.
I slowly realize all of my lies,
And like a child I am chastised.
I pick up a pen and paper 8 X 11 size.
First sentence;
Sister I apologize.

Kawan D. Fields Used by Permission

Endless Pain

From the darkness
an explosion.
My mind copies
the displayed convulsion.
As time stops
it starts corrosion
Among chaos;
the constant implosion,
"What have I done?"

The heart stops
the moment sight lands;
Cain stares down
while Abel no long stands.
My soul's voice low,
feeling drips from my hands,
Conscience fleeing
through a beach of guilt sands...
What have I done?

Sleep absent,
leaving fearful reality;
haunted within
by my own morality.
Sentenced to life
by evil sensuality,
Search for solace,
trapped by technicality.
What have I done?

In my darkness
a painful light revealed;
heart bursting with grief,
never shall be healed.
With release of the bullets,
two fates sealed.
I didn't take one
but two lives I've killed.
What have I done?

Kawan D. Fields Used by Permission

Book Appendix

Letters of Support

Michigan Department of Corrections

Certifications of Achievement

Parole Board and Commutation

Original - Cour 1st copy - Co. ons 2nd copy - Corrections (or return) 3rd copy - Arresting agency

STATE OF MICHIGAN ~~JUDICIAL CIRCUIT~~ RECORDER'S COURT	**JUDGMENT OF SENTENCE** Commitment To Corrections Department	CASE NO. 84 0868

Court address: 1441 St. Antoine, Detroit, Michigan 48226

Court telephone no.: 224-5531

THE PEOPLE OF THE STATE OF MICHIGAN v

Defendant name and address: DAVID K. HUDSON

SID:

DOB: 7-16-58 BM

Prosecuting attorney name: JOHN D. O'HAIR — Bar no.: P 18432

Defendant attorney name: STUART YOUNG — Bar no.: P 22654

1. At a session on 4-24-85 (Date), Recorder's ~~Circuit~~ Court Judge MICHAEL F. SAPALA, P. 19891 (Bar no.) presiding:

2. THE COURT FINDS that the defendant, represented by counsel, was found guilty on 4-11-85 (Date) of the crime(s) as stated below.

Count	CONVICTED BY Plea*	Court	Jury	CRIME	CCH	MCL Specify section and sub section
1			G	MURDER FIRST DEGREE		750.316
2			G	ROBBERY ARMED		750.529
3			G	POSSESSION OF A FIREARM		750.227B

*Plea: insert "G" for guilty plea; use "NC" for nolo contendere

IT IS ORDERED:

3. Defendant is sentenced to the custody of the Michigan Department of Corrections as stated below. This sentence shall be immediately executed.

Count	SENTENCE DATE	MINIMUM Years	Mos.	Days	MAXIMUM Years	Mos.	DATE SENTENCE BEGINS	JAIL CREDIT Mos.	Days	OTHER INFORMATION
1	4-24-85	LIFE					1-28-86	0	0	
2	4-24-85	CONVICTION SET ASIDE BY THE COURT (DOUBLE JEOPARDY)								
3	4-24-85	2	0	0	2	0	4-24-85	0	452	

Court recommendation:

Michael F. Sapala

~~Circuit Court Judge~~ MICHAEL F. SAPALA
JUDGE OF RECORDER'S COURT

I certify that this is a correct and complete abstract from the original court records. The sheriff shall, without needless delay, deliver defendant to the Michigan Department of Corrections at a place designated by the department.

(SEAL) Diana Gist — Deputy Court Clerk — 16a

Approved, State Court Administrator 4/84

JUDGMENT OF SENTENCE, COMMITMENT TO CORRECTIONS DEPARTMENT — Form No. CC 219b (4 part)

STATE OF MICHIGAN
DEPARTMENT OF CORRECTIONS
LANSING

JENNIFER M. GRANHOLM
GOVERNOR

PATRICIA L. CARUSO
DIRECTOR

January 23, 2009

Mr. Avern Cohn, District Judge
United States District Court
Eastern District of Michigan
Theodore Levin United States Courthouse
231 West Lafayette-Room 219
Detroit, MI 48226

Dear Mr. Cohn:

This letter acknowledges receipt of your letter to the Michigan Parole Board regarding the Application for Pardon or Commutation of Sentence for David Hudson #179401.

Our records show that a commutation of sentence application was received in our office on June 13, 2008. On December 12, 2008, it was sent to the Governor's office for her consideration. It is confirmed that your letter dated September 23, 2008, was included with the application.

Sincerely,

MICHIGAN PAROLE BOARD

jlg

GRANDVIEW PLAZA BUILDING • P.O. BOX 30003 • LANSING, MICHIGAN 48909
www.michigan.gov • (517) 335-1426

UNITED STATES DISTRICT COURT
EASTERN DISTRICT OF MICHIGAN
THEODORE LEVIN UNITED STATES COURTHOUSE
231 WEST LAFAYETTE- ROOM 219
DETROIT, MICHIGAN 48226

(313) 234-5160

CHAMBERS OF
AVERN COHN
DISTRICT JUDGE

e-mail: avern_cohn@mied.uscourts.gov

October 30, 2012

Michigan Parole Board
Office of the Parole Board
Michigan Department of Corrections
P.O. Box 30003
Lansing, MI 48909

Re: Commutation Petition of David Hudson
ID #A179401

Dear Parole Board Members:

I understand that David Hudson has again applied for a commutation of his life sentence. I was the judge to whom Mr. Hudson applied for a writ of habeas corpus on the grounds his constitutional rights were violated in his state court trial. I agreed with Mr. Hudson, granted the writ, and instructed the state court to retry the case. The Court of Appeals for the Sixth Circuit in a 2 to 1 decision disagreed, reversing my decision.

I wrote you previously on September 28, 2008. A copy of the letter is enclosed.

Again based on what I know I believe Mr. Hudson is a worthy candidate for serious consideration for commutation of his sentence.

I also ask that you include this letter in your report to the Governor on Mr. Hudson's petition.

Sincerely,

Avern Cohn

AC:jao

cc: Mr. David Hudson

encl

EIVED
MI DEPT . CORRECTIONS

;12760

AUG 0 6 2008

PAROLE BOARD

MICHIGAN SENATE
410 FARNUM
P.O. BOX 30036
LANSING, MI 48909-7536
PHONE: (517) 373-7315
TOLL-FREE: (866) 303-0110
FAX: (517) 373-3126
DISTRICT: (586) 774-2430
E-MAIL: senmswitalski@senate.michigan.gov

MICHAEL SWITALSKI

STATE SENATOR
10TH DISTRICT
CLINTON TOWNSHIP · ROSEVILLE · STERLING HEIGHTS · UTICA

APPROPRIATIONS COMMITTEE
MINORITY VICE CHAIR
SUBCOMMITTEES:
CAPITAL OUTLAY, (MVC)
K-12, SCHOOL AID, EDUCATION, (MVC)
COMMUNITY HEALTH
SENATE FISCAL AGENCY
BOARD OF GOVERNORS

July 24, 2008

Governor Jennifer M. Granholm
ATTN: Kelly Keenan, Esq.
George M. Romney Building
P.O. Box 30013
Lansing, Michigan 48909

VIA ID MAIL

RE: David K. Hudson #A179401
Ryan Correctional Facility
17600 Ryan Road
Detroit, Michigan 48212

Dear Mr. Keenan:

I understand that you have received or will receive an Application for Commutation of Sentence from David K. Hudson, a prisoner at the Ryan Correctional Facility. I support this prisoner's commutation.

I met David last year when I spoke to the National Lifers Association Chapter at the Ryan Correctional Facility. David was very helpful in making my visit productive. I again met David when I attended the closing ceremony for the Inside-Out Prison Exchange Program at Ryan. The Inside-Out Prison Exchange Program is where students and prisoners attend class together within the prison to study criminal justice issues. During my talks with him, I found David to be very articulate and eloquent.

Because he knows education is extremely important, he has taken advantage of many educational opportunities while in prison. In addition to taking part in the Inside-Out Prison Exchange Program, David has received certificates in paralegal studies, A+ computer refurbishing, and custodial maintenance. Based upon his educational background, David should be very employable upon his release.

Thank you for considering my support for David K. Hudson's commutation. If you have any questions or concerns about David, please do not hesitate to contact me.

Sincerely,

Michael Switalski
State Senator
10th District

JEANICE DAGHER-MARGOSIAN
ATTORNEY
Ann Arbor, MI

7.24.08

Michigan Parole Board
POB 30003
Lansing, MI 48909

RE: Commutation Petition of David Hudson, #A179401

To the Members of the Board:

I am a member of the Michigan Bar, writing on behalf of Mr. Hudson and to express my support for his release.

My acquaintance with Mr. Hudson commenced when I began representing him on his criminal appeal in the Michigan Courts. This was approximately 1996. I continued to represent him through the Supreme Court and on habeas review in the federal courts.

I was deeply aware, throughout representation of Mr. Hudson, of the imbalance of state power against the unsophisticated young man in this case, that was operative from the day of his arrest. Few cases in my long career have impressed me so profoundly in their unconstitutional and cold treatment of a suspected offender. He was 19 or 20, I believe, at the time this arrest took place. He was held at the Detroit Police Department for many hours, locked in a small room, and chained to a desk, if I remember correctly. He did not have much experience with the criminal justice system. I remember that he tried to tell authorities that he wanted an attorney, and he tried to have his family contact an attorney. His requests were roundly ignored.

Mr. Hudson went to trial unprepared to meet the armory of the State's forces against him. I remember that this was a trial with what I felt were many viable claims of error. Unfortunately, the Michigan appellate courts did not find that these claims supported relief in the form of a new trial or vacated conviction.

The fact that habeas relief was later granted in the Federal District Court, Eastern District, demonstrates the injustice that remains forever a part of his conviction. Structural error was found by the Court due to trial proceedings which did not properly include defense participation. This was later reversed by

1

the Sixth Circuit, but there was a spirited and cogent dissent. It is very regrettable that Mr. Hudson did not get the relief that he truly deserved.

As an individual, Mr. Hudson is extremely intelligent and diligent in his intellectual efforts. As the Board is aware, he has spent years studying the law and litigating on behalf of himself and others who have no other voice. He is focused and very strong about what he believes. I am also sure that now, with a history of intellectual and legal activism, as a man in mid-life with grandchildren, there is certainly no question of recidivism. Common sense indicates this. Research indicates the same. Accordingly, there is no purpose that I can see to continuing to incarcerate Mr. Hudson at a cost to myself and other taxpayers of about $25,000 per year.

Sincerely,

Jeanice Dagher-Margosian

BRIAN K. LAWSON

3543 GLENN DR. S.E.
GRAND RAPIDS, MI 49546

Office of The Governor
c/o Kelly Keenan
Legal Counsel to the Governor
Lansing, MI 48909

October 9, 2008

Dear Governor Granholm:

In re: Petition for Commutation for David Hudson
Inmate #A179401

Several years ago, I was asked by a Federal Magistrate in the Western District of Michigan to assist an inmate who, on behalf of himself and others similarly situated, was being denied the right to observe his religion. That inmate was David Hudson.

David was my first "prisoner's rights" case, so I was not sure what to expect. Mr. Hudson was, from the first moment we met, respectful, kind and dignified. He evinced the commitment and intelligence that had allowed him to prepare his case in an impressive fashion. Throughout our relationship, he displayed a maturity and reasonableness that belied his situation, and at all times he was as concerned with the plight of others as he was about his own. He approached the case with a reasonable, practical perspective, and when the case ended, Mr. Hudson was genuinely appreciative. I could not have asked for a better client.

I cannot claim to know David extremely well. What I do know of him, though, suggests that he has taken responsibility for his past, and that he has gone to tremendous pains to improve his situation, while helping others along the way.

I could not help but notice the respect shown David by both his fellow inmates and the guards, a respect borne from decades of good behavior and a commitment to the cause of helping his fellow inmates. I have no doubt that, if given a chance, David would be one of those people dedicated to making sure others do not follow the path that led him to prison. For that reason, I hope you will strongly consider commuting Mr. Hudson's sentence and allow him to take his talents into the community.

Very truly yours,

Brian K. Lawson

Document1.bkl

DEPARTMENT OF BEHAVIORAL SCIENCES

UNIVERSITY OF MICHIGAN-DEARBORN
COLLEGE OF ARTS, SCIENCES AND LETTERS

4901 EVERGREEN ROAD
DEARBORN, MICHIGAN 48128-1491
313-593-5520 FAX 313-583-6358

April 28, 2008

To: Governor Jennifer M. Granholm
State of Michigan
George M. Romney Building
P.O. Box 30013
Lansing, MI 48909

Michigan Parole Board
206 East Michigan Avenue
PO Box 30003
Lansing, MI 48909

From: Lora Bex Lempert, Ph.D.
Professor in Sociology and Women's and Gender Studies
University of Michigan - Dearborn

Re: David Keith Hudson 179401

Dear Governor Granholm and Parole Board Members:

It is with great enthusiasm and uncompromising hope that I write in support of David Hudson's petition for commutation. Mr. Hudson is currently an inmate at Ryan Correctional Facility. He has been incarcerated for twenty four years.

I make this recommendation for his release without qualification. I have known Mr. Hudson for several years and I can speak confidently and informatively of his readiness to reintegrate into life outside prison. In the many years of his incarceration, he has transformed himself from a young man who was reactive rather than proactive into a mature adult who has gained the "wisdom that suffering brings," i.e., the suffering that he caused as well as the suffering that he has endured in 24 years of incarceration. He has accepted the personal consequences of his bad choices, grieved deeply for the consequences to others, and set about to build a better life for himself and others within imposed confines of the prison context.

I first met David Hudson in 2003 when he was the Program Director for the National Lifers of America (NLA) at Ryan. I am a co-sponsor of Chapter 1014 at Scott Correctional. Mr. Hudson invited me to speak to the national on the topic of "Gender in Prison." This was a first for all of us. Mr. Hudson took care of all the administrative requirements – time, space, procedures for clearance, and so on – and acted as my host for the day. In each of these tasks, he demonstrated an ease, competence, and a quiet dignity. It was also immediately clear that David Hudson was held in high esteem by his peers and that many deferred to his judgment and perspectives.

In 2007, Mr. Hudson was elected President of the national NLA. In this role, he organized the first in the state Legislative Town Meeting held inside a correctional facility to discuss carceral issues. State Senators Smith, Condino, Johnson, and Jackson were all in attendance. He has also organized numerous Legislative and Legal seminars to foster understandings between policy makers outside the prisons and inmates living with the policy decisions. Local attorneys, state senators, council persons from Detroit, and state appellate defenders have all participated.

Most recently, my contact with David Hudson was frequent and continuous as he was a student of mine in an historical, first time in Michigan, university course that combined 15 university students ("outside students") and 15 inmates ("Inside Students") in the same class in Ryan Correctional. Inside-Out Prison Exchange is a community-based, University of Michigan – Dearborn approved, curricular course. Together students explore issues of crime and justice, drawing on one another to create a deeper understanding of how these issues affect our lives as individuals and as a society. The course creates a dynamic partnership between UMD and Ryan Correctional to allow students to question approaches to issues of crime and justice in order to build a safer and more just society for all. The course encourages outside students to contextualize and to think deeply about what they have learned about crime and criminals and to help them pursue the work of creating a restorative criminal justice system; it challenges inside students to place their life experiences into larger social contexts and to rekindle their intellectual self-confidence and interest in further education.

The class met weekly Fall Semester 2007 with a Completion Ceremony, attended by State Senators Alan Cropsey, Michael Switalski, and Hansen Clarke, and State Representative Alma Wheeler Smith in December 2007. Because the class is so unique in its population and climate, I came to know each of the students very well. David was always present, actively listening and thoughtfully considering the contributions of all his peers before he volunteered his own analyses. He is an intellectually curious student, always prepared, and always ready to engage new ideas and perspectives. The course directs attention to alternative interpretations of the experiences that resulted in imprisonment, moving from personal experience to social context through analyses of past and present socio-cultural circumstances. It was my intent that the course would move students towards an understanding of the social forces that have shaped their lives. In this discourse, David Hudson was particularly insightful. His course contributions were many – he role modeled for all the students an active intellectual engagement with course content. His reading journal entries were among the best I've read from any student Inside or Outside; they were creative and they demonstrated a blend of academic motivation and personal responsibility that make him an ideal candidate for renewed citizenship "outside" of prison.

David Hudson is no longer the young man who was sentenced in 1984, who early on in his life made some extraordinarily bad decisions, and who was reactive to his life circumstances. I have been impressed since the time of my first meeting with David by the depth of his understandings and perceptions of his, and other men's, decision-making processes. More than many other inmates, David Hudson has used his time in prison to think about, to analyze, to change, and, perhaps most importantly, to "own" his choices.

To say that Mr. Hudson is a role model understates the respect that he engenders in other inmates. More accurately, he is a magnet, particularly in his position as HIV/AIDS counselor. He has committed his energies to informing, to educating, and to protecting men from the ravages of this communicable disease. He is also a certified paralegal; a certified computer refurbisher; and is certified in custodial maintenance by Schoolcraft College.

These "self-improvement" opportunities situate him well for success after parole. He is educated; he is self aware. Most assuredly, he is motivated to succeed.
He has a supportive family structure that will facilitate his transition to life "outside." Additionally, David Hudson is a bright, talented, and capable person. He does not live on illusion; he is practical and pragmatic. He will not be a recidivist. He is no danger to anyone.

David Hudson is both a role model and mentor to young men in the carceral system. He serves as a role model for other prisoners precisely because he has shed neither his identity nor his sense of himself as a person willing and able to make valuable contributions.

I have no doubt that he will become a contributing member of society upon parole. His already lengthy incarceration has served the purpose of punishment, as well as rehabilitation. Further incarceration cannot offer additional remediation for this man who has already acquired the "wisdom" that many never achieve. It would be punishment without purpose.

At the University of Michigan – Dearborn, we would be pleased to have David Hudson apply to complete his education. We would welcome his application to the SOAR Program, a program designed to assist re-entry students with academic support.

I strongly urge the committee to grant David Keith Hudson a commutation of sentence.

Should you require further information from me, please contact me at 313 593 5520 or at llempert@umd.umich.edu.

Sincerely,

Lora Lempert /rab

Lora Lempert, Ph.D.

LL/rab

UNIVERSITY OF MICHIGAN
DEPARTMENT OF ENGLISH LANGUAGE AND LITERATURE

October 31, 2008

RECEIVED
MI DEPT of CORRECTIONS

NOV 10 2008

PAROLE BOARD

Ms. Barbara Sampson
Chairperson, Office of the Parole Board
Grandview Plaza Building
PO Box 30003, 206 E. Michigan Avenue
Lansing, Michigan 48909

Dear Ms. Sampson,

Bishop William H. Murphy, Jr., has filed a Petition for Commutation on behalf of David Hudson (#A179401, and I am writing in support of that petition. I have sent this same letter to Governor Granholm.

In 1990 I founded the Prison Creative Arts Project (PCAP) at the University of Michigan. Since that time, PCAP has provided the Michigan Department of Corrections with over 400 workshop programs in the arts. Urban high school youth and incarcerated youth and adults, working with us, have created 486 original plays since 1990 and since 1996 we have curated thirteen Annual Exhibitions of Art by Michigan Prisoners, leading to the most extensive production of artistic work in any prison system in this country. PCAP is a nationally recognized organization. In 2005 I was awarded the Carnegie Foundation for the Improvement of Education and Council for the Advancement and Support of Education Professor of the Year Award, which led to a Special Tribute by the Ninety-Third Michigan State Legislature, a recognition of the achievements of our challenged urban youth and our incarcerated young and adult citizens and of the University of Michigan students who have participated in PCAP.

In 1992 the inmates at Western Wayne Correctional Facility who had just finished their first play decided to create an original play based on their own paths to prison and intended for at-risk youth incarcerated at Maxey Boys Training School and elsewhere. Thanks to the support of the warden and of the Michigan Department of Corrections a professional video team was able to film "Inside Out," which was used in an video interaction between Adrian Training School and the five actors remaining at Western Wayne. The film also received some distribution to youth facilities around the country and to some college campuses. I worked with the group for an entire year as they worked on the film, and at some point early on, Mr. Hudson joined the group. He was committed, large-spirited, fully dedicated to getting a message to the youth, and generous both with his input into the content of "Inside Out" and in his interaction with and collaboration with the others. He brought both seriousness and humor to the work, a combination that kept the group steady and relaxed as they went into some hard places in their lives. He was transferred before we began the actual filming, but a personal story that he contributed – for the two scenes on family and drugs – remained in the play and was one of the more powerful segments.

He later joined a theater workshop facilitated by two of my students at the Gus Harrison Correctional Facility, and was constantly praised by the two – his maturity, his understanding of the process, his dedication to themes that helped the prison audience think about their lives in positive ways were invaluable contributions.

3187 ANGELL HALL • ANN ARBOR MI 48109-1003 • PHONE: 734.764.6330 • FAX: 734.763.3128 • http://www.lsa.umich.edu/english

Since then, once Mr. Hudson rose to leadership in the Lifers Associations at the facilities where he has been incarcerated, he has not had time to participate in our programs (in those facilities where we actually had some available), but I received communications from him asking if the Prison Creative Arts Projects could bring programs to the Lifers Association – I had letters that I recall from both the Saginaw Correctional Facility and the Ryan Correctional Facility. And from what I read of his record, this represents his work, always seeking active programming that will support rehabilitation efforts at whatever facility he was resident, including bringing to the Ryan Facility the Pennsylvania Inside Out Program in which inmates take classes through the University of Michigan Dearborn and earn credits if they pursue their education after release, including the recent Legislative Town Hall meeting at the Ryan Facility, including seminars with the Reconciliation of Life Ministry, including involving other inmates in fundraising programs for charitable organizations. He has supported other prisoners as a paralegal and as a mentor. Mr. Hudson came to a recent performance by one of the PCAP workshops at the Ryan Facility and we were able to talk a little. I was pleased to learn how much he has contributed during his incarceration and to find myself talking with an even more mature and dedicated person than I had known personally back at the Western Wayne Correctional Facility.

During the days at Western Wayne, I came to know Dr. Charles Harper and the work he did in group and individual therapy that turned around another inmate, who went on afterwards to complete both an undergraduate and a graduate degree (in the School of Social Work) at the University of Michigan. I see in the materials that Mr. Hudson has sent me that Dr. Harper wrote in his termination report that "David used therapy to foster personal growth in his life has been nothing short of phenomenal... he can be expected to become a leader in his community and make a major contribution." The Dr. Harper I know is highly responsible and sure and does not exaggerate. His assessment reflects everything I believe about Mr. Hudson.

We in the Prison Creative Arts Project remain committed to the inmates we have worked with when they come home. We have a Linkage Project in which we connect former inmates with community arts mentors in the cities or towns they return to. Mr. Hudson would be a prime candidate for this Project. I will also be personally supportive of him in any way I can.

Sincerely,

Buzz Alexander
Founder of the Prison Creative Arts Project
Thurnau Professor of English, University of Michigan

Bishop William H. Murphy Jr.
New Mount Moriah International Church
313 E. Walton Blvd.
Pontiac, MI 48340
248-332- 3070
www.williammurphyministries.org

Dear Governor Granholm,

Attached is a petition for commutation signed by me on behalf of David K. Hudson #A179401.

Due to the fact that the state is releasing those who have serves time and is no longer a threat to society. I am recommending David for consideration for an early release. This could be done by reducing David's life sentence to 15 to 30 years. David has served already nearly 25 years. I have known David for many years and understand that life's issues placed David in the wrong company at the wrong time and place.

David's time in incarceration has afforded him many achievements and accomplishments (Attached is a Copy). David has proven in his time of incarceration that he can and will be a positive force in society if given the chance. We have found through research that there are many who have been in the same circumstances that have not been given the same level of sentence. Prior to his incarceration David have not been in any trouble with law enforcement.

David has a stable family at home and at church with those who are willing to help and assistant in his transition. As president of the National Lifers of America Inc., David recently hosted seminars with State Representatives Alma Wheeler Smith, State Rep. Paul Condino, and State Senator Hansen Clark, Senator Michael "Mickey Switalski, Senator Alan Cropsey and Mayor K. Kilpatrick, among others. Several of these legislators have shared dinner with David at Ryan Road Facility through the U of M *Inside Out Program.*

Governor, America is a land of second chances. I believe that David is a prime candidate who has earned and merits a second chance. He has shown and expressed remorse for these crimes in our counseling session at Ryan Road. I firmly believe through our consultations and my personal knowledge, David is no longer a risk to society and will be a productive member. Thank you for any serous consideration you give in the most important matter.

Sincerely,

Bishop William H. Murphy Jr.

DANESHA LYNN PAUL
Notary Public, State of Michigan
County of Oakland
My Commission Expires Mar. 09, 2013
Acting In the County of Oakland

4632 McDougall
Detroit, MI 48207
313-924-7340

Evangelist: Lucille Steele

July 30, 2008

Michigan Parole Board
206 East Michigan Avenue
P.O. Box 30013
Lansing, MI 48909
DAVID HUDSON #A179401

RECEIVED
MI DEPT of CORRECTIONS
AUG 1 4 2003
PAROLE BOARD

Dear Parole Board Members:

This letter is being written concerning the petition for commutation for Mr. David Hudson, who is currently an inmate at the Ryan Correctional Facility. Mr. Hudson has as of this time been incarcerated for the past twenty-four years.

I have known David Hudson from birth and have known his family since before his birth. His parents and I all belonged to the same Church, "New Salem Baptist Church" and we raised our children up together while attending services there. Great individuals who tried to instill in him good morals and values raised David Hudson. I know this to be true because I was one of those individuals.

We try to give our children all of the tools that they will need to succeed out in the world and pray that all we have given them will be enough to sustain them. We try to protect them from the outside forces that seem to draw them into their nets, but sometimes those drawing powers are stronger than even a parent staunch warning. Those outside forces found their way into David's life and in a blink of ones eye many lives were changed.

Those of us who knew David before this tragedy, could not believe that this young man of whom we had all had a hand in raising could be a part of anything like what he was being accused of. We rallied around him and supported his family in anyway that we could, because they were whom we knew. As Christian we also had to send up our prayers and love for all of the individuals who were a part of this tragedy that we did not know, but who were paining and suffering from their losses. We continue to pray for all the individuals who were drawn into this tragedy for whatever reason and we continue to ask God to wrap His ever-loving and strong arms around each of us. I continue to be a part of David's life today. I continue to visit him and bring the word of God into his life as well as what is happening within our family's lives, because we all need to know that someone is in our corner, even when that corner seems so small that no one but you can fit in it.

July 30, 2008
Page 2

It is because of my belief in God that I can write each of you this letter and ask for all of your considerations in Mr. David Hudson commutation. Since his incarceration, over the past twenty-four years David has grown into a man of substance. He has expressed his remorse for any and all involvement in the tragedy's of his past. He has gone back to school and has done quite well for himself. He is as of this year continuing to take college courses in order to stay abreast of the current events of the world.

David is involved in many positive programs inside of the prison facility such as, the community based, University of Michigan, Inside-Out Prison Exchange program. David is also the "Program Director for National Lifers of America" (NLA).

Mr. David Hudson can be a model for rehabilitation, for he has thrown himself into turning his life around and becoming someone who can be trusted to return back into society and become an upright citizen who anyone would be proud to be around and everyone will feel safe to live around.

It is with my sincere belief in David's heartfelt remorse and full rehabilitation that I write to each of you and request that all of you dig deep into your hearts and find the strength to give a man who has shown that he can change, by actually changing another chance at experiencing freedom.

Sincerely,

Mrs. Lucille Steele
Evangelist

000379

Reconciliation of Life Ministries
P.O. Box 6853
Grand Rapids, MI 49516-6853
(616) 241-3396

April 13, 2004

Mr. Charles Braddaock
Michigan Parole Board
P.O. Box 30003
Lansing, MI 48909

Re: Commutation, David Hudson #179401

Dear Mr. Braddaock:

My name is Sister Wanda Rogers. I am the Founder and Director of the Ministry of Reconciliation of Life which provides prison visitation transportation. I am writing this letter in regards to Mr. David Hudson's commutation.

Mr. Hudson has been supporting our work here in Grand Rapids for the last three years. His Organization F.I.N.D. (Fathers Incarcerated Needing to be Dad), has sent clocks by mail for fund raisers at their own expense. They have offered to help our homeless shelters in Grand Rapids with boxes of cosmetics. Mr. Hudson has been a big support to my husband's coming into the prison system and speaking to the men in Saginaw.

Now that I have spoken about a few of the things that Mr. Hudson is doing within the prison walls, let me now speak in Biblical terms. We know that Mr. Hudson committed murder, but so did Paul, one of God's best disciples. Paul was a man who killed God's people just because he had the power to do so. Before his name was changed, he was Saul, the persecutor of the Church. Before you make a determination, please read Acts, chapters 8 and 9 in your Bible. Mr. Braddaock, Paul's sentence should have been death. But had God executed him or left him in prison for life, he would not have been able to start the many churches for the cause of Christ after God saved him. God does not hang our sins over our heads for life. Jesus died that all man could be reconciled. 2 Corinthians 5:19, "To wit, that God was in Christ, reconciling the world unto himself, not imputing their trespasses unto them; and hath committed unto us the word of reconciliation." I, myself, was once a prisoner of crime (sin) but now I am a servant of God, serving his people.

If you have any questions, please feel free to call me at the number above.

May God bless you,

Sister Wanda Rogers

Sister Wanda Rogers,
Founder, Director

6-24-06

ACKNOWLEDGED
by Postcard
Date: 6/28/06 BM

To Whom it may Concern;

This Letter is in reference to the Moral character of David Hudson #179401 Ryan Facility.
I am a Deacon in the church that has known said inmate for the Last 22 years.
I can speak to the intigrity of David by saying that he is a changed person for the better.

Any consideration that you could render toward the possible release of David would be greatly appreciated.

Thank You

Deacon Joseph Lateef

RECEIVED
JUN 26 2006

Michigan Department of Corrections

"Expecting Excellence Every Day"

Memorandum

DATE: March 13, 2012

TO: David Hudson, #179401, C-3-04

FROM: Warden Carol Howes
Lakeland Correctional Facility

SUBJECT: Commendation

I am writing to commend you for being a positive influence and role model at Lakeland. It is difficult to believe that you have been at Lakeland for only 2 ½ years considering your accomplishments.

You have been a full time dog trainer, involved in Chance for Life programs, and served on the Warden's Forum. You have still found time to write and publish a book, Gangsta Rap for the Youth. Your book is an inspiration. It will cause readers to stop and think about consequences of the choices they make in life.

Through all the negativity that comes with living in prison, you have managed to find a positive purpose in life.

cc: Record Office file

STATE OF MICHIGAN
DEPARTMENT OF CORRECTIONS
LAKELAND/FLORENCE CRANE CORRECTIONAL FACILITIES & CAMP BRANCH

JENNIFER M. GRANHOLM
GOVERNOR

PATRICIA L. CARUSO
DIRECTOR

August 23, 2010

David Hudson-Bey #179401 C-3-48
Lakeland Correctional Facility

Dear Mr. Hudson-Bey:

This correspondence is prepared in recognition of the fine work you did recently in co-coordinating with Mr. Etchison-Bey, the National Lifer's of America Inc., Legislative Issues seminar on August 21, 2010 at the Lakeland Correctional Facility.

Your efforts are reflective of the type of community service that contributes to the improvement of the quality of life for staff as well as prisoners within the confines of a correctional facility.

Your contribution to productive programming is appreciated.

Sincerely,

Dan Hawkins
~~ADW Programs~~/Housing
Lakeland Correctional Facility

DH:blp
NLA Hudson-Bey #179401
cc: Warden Howes
Deputy Warden Hoffner
ARUS Marvin
Counselor File

141 FIRST STREET • COLDWATER, MICHIGAN 49036
www.michigan.gov • (517) 278-6942

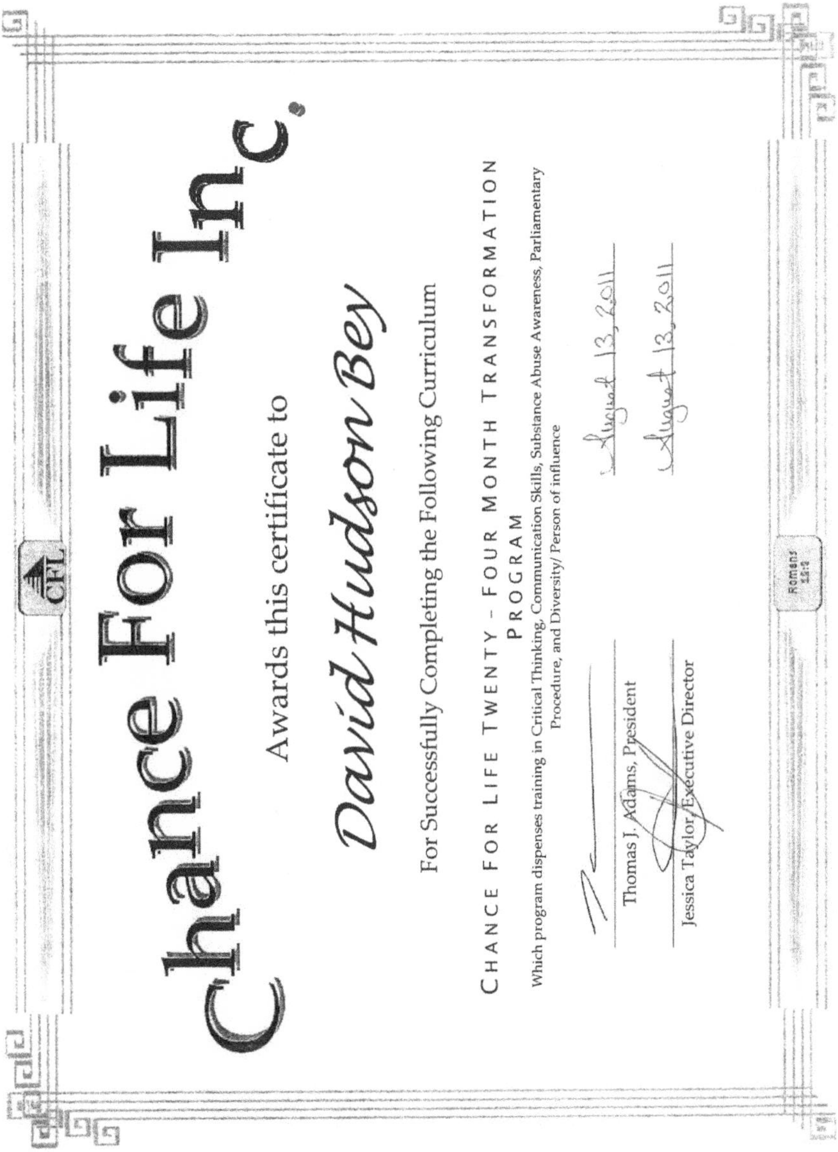

CFL

Chance For Life Inc.

Awards this certificate to

David Hudson Bey

For Successfully Completing the Following Curriculum

CHANCE FOR LIFE TWENTY - FOUR MONTH TRANSFORMATION PROGRAM

Which program dispenses training in Critical Thinking, Communication Skills, Substance Abuse Awareness, Parliamentary Procedure, and Diversity/ Person of influence

Thomas J. Adams, President — August 13, 2011

Jessica Taylor, Executive Director — August 13, 2011

Romans 15:13

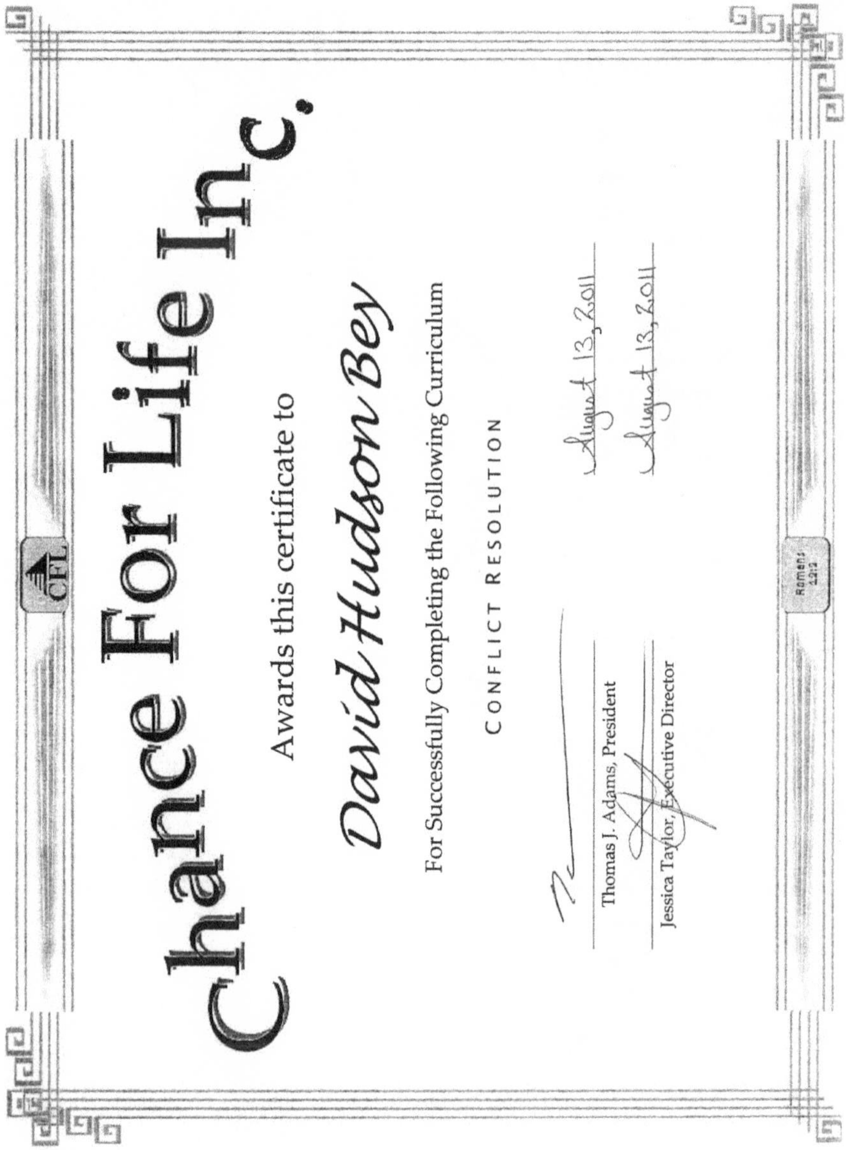

CFL

Chance For Life Inc.

Awards this certificate to

David Hudson Bey

For Successfully Completing the Following Curriculum

CONFLICT RESOLUTION

Thomas J. Adams, President — August 13, 2011

Jessica Taylor, Executive Director — August 13, 2011

Romans

CHANCE FOR LIFE ORGANIZATION

This certificate is awarded to

DAVID K. HUDSON BEY

For Successfully Completing the Following CFL Classes

COMMUNICATION SKILLS ~ PARENTING & MENTORING SKILLS ~
SUBSTANCE ABUSE AWARENESS ~ CRITICAL THINKING

Thomas J. Adams, President 4-28-10

Jessica Taylor, Executive Director 4-28-10

CFL

The University of Michigan – Dearborn
College of Arts, Sciences, and Letters

presents this Certificate of Completion

to

David Keith Hudson

in recognition of having successfully completed

Inside Out Prison Exchange

this fourteenth day of December, two thousand and seven.

Continuing Education Units (CEUs) Awarded: 3.9

Kathryn Anderson-Levitt
Dean
College of Arts, Sciences, and Letters
The University of Michigan – Dearborn

Lora Lempert
Program Coordinator
College of Arts, Sciences, and Letters
The University of Michigan – Dearborn

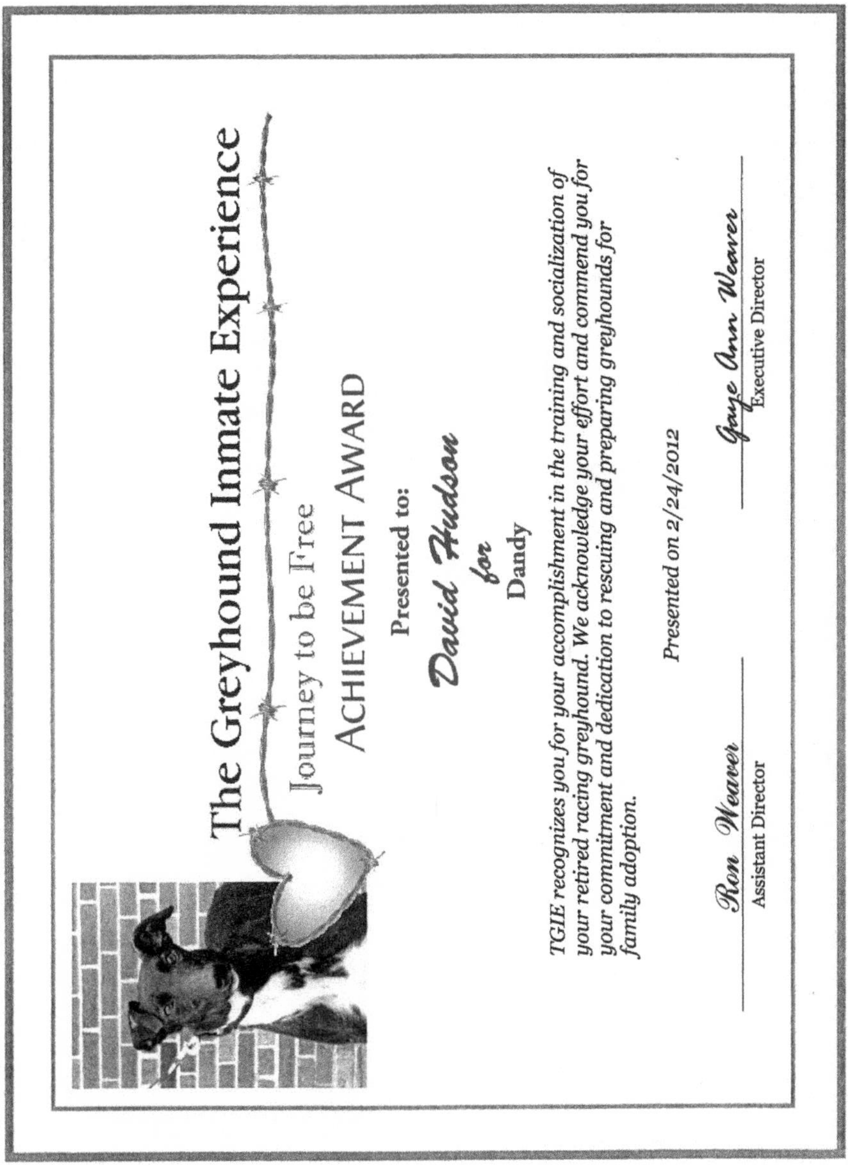

The Greyhound Inmate Experience

Journey to be Free

ACHIEVEMENT AWARD

Presented to:

David Hudson

for

Dandy

TGIE recognizes you for your accomplishment in the training and socialization of your retired racing greyhound. We acknowledge your effort and commend you for your commitment and dedication to rescuing and preparing greyhounds for family adoption.

Presented on 2/24/2012

Ron Weaver
Assistant Director

Gaye Ann Weaver
Executive Director

MICHIGAN DEPARTMENT OF CORRECTIONS

PRISONER PROGRAM AND WORK ASSIGNMENT EVALUATION

CSJ-363
REV. 09/06
4835-3363

Prisoner Name (last)	(first)	(middle initial)	Prisoner No.	Lock No.	Institution Code
Hudson	David		179401	C-3-4	LCF
Assignment Name			Assignment No.	Date Assigned	Date Evaluated
The Greyhound Inmate Experience - Dog Handler				9/6/11	10/7/13
Assignment Classification: ☐ Student ☐ Unskilled ☐ Semi-Skilled ☒ Skilled ☐ Other			Race NW	Date Terminated	Will Take Back ☒ Yes ☐ No

Circle the number beside each statement which describes the prisoner's work/school assignment performance:	3 or more exceptions	1-2 exceptions	No exceptions
1. The prisoner was on time.	0	2	(3)
2. The prisoner came on the correct days.	0	2	(3)
3. The prisoner followed all safety rules.	0	2	(3)
4. The prisoner followed all other rules.	0	2	(3)
5. The prisoner followed the assignment authority's instructions.	0	2	(3)
6. The prisoner cooperated with the assignment authority, followed the working chain of command and refrained from arguing about assignments. (Working relationship with Authority)	0	2	(3)
7. The prisoner discussed work/education related problems with peers/tutor, listened to peer's/tutor's point of view, encouraged discussion without argument and limited disruptive vocalizations. (Communication with Peers)	0	2	(3)
8. The prisoner did the assignment share of the work/education assignment, remained in the assigned area until the end of the shift and engaged in no horseplay. (Teamwork with Peers)	0	2	(3)
9. The prisoner kept a neat, clean and well groomed personal appearance, suitable for the assignment.	0	2	(3)
10. The prisoner did job/education tasks according to the job/education description.	0	2	(3)
11. The prisoner kept the work area neat and clean.	0	2	(3)
12. The prisoner worked without constant supervision or direction when appropriate.	0	2	(3)
13. The prisoner was willing to perform additional duties or stay beyond scheduled time. When asked, the prisoner did not argue or complain and performed additional assignments in a satisfactory manner.	0	2	(3)
REVIEWED: Prisoner's Signature: Date:	COLUMN TOTAL:		39
I RECOMMEND:	TOTAL SCORE:	39	

☐ Entry Pay with 30 Days Conditional · Below Average Score 0-27 ☐ Status Pay Satisfactory · Average Score 28-34
☐ * Above Average Score 35-39 ☐ Bonus Pay for Food Service Workers ☐ Termination ☐ Close Supervision

Fill in the appropriate information for school programming ** No notations in the 3 or more exceptions column.*

14. Academic CBI Modules in Progress ☐ N/A — Subject; Letter/Number / / / / /

15. GED Test Version | I | II | III | IV | V | Avg. Standard Score | Date Tested

16. Voc Ed Program in Progress ☐ N/A — Duties (capital letter) Completed. If duty not complete, print duty letter & task (number) completed.

17. Pre-Release/Job Seeking Skills Completed ☐ YES ☐ NO — Date Completed:

18. Completed training to operate the following machinery or equipment: — Date Completed:

19. Attendance — Hours Attended — Hours Missed

COMMENTS AND RECOMMENDATIONS:

Mr. Hudson has been a Dog Handler for the Greyhound Inmate Experience for over two years. He has been a valuable part of the team demonstrating dedication, patience, skilled training and teamwork. Thank you for making this program a success!

BE POSITIVE, STAY FOCUSED, REMAIN COMMITTED!

Evaluator's Signature	Supervisor's Signature
Evaluator's Printed Name and Title	Supervisor's Printed Name and Title
ARUS A. Houtz	A/RUM Morrell

DISTRIBUTION: White – Record Office; Green – Assignment Supervisor; Canary – School Principal/Classification Director; Pink – RUM; Goldenrod – Prisoner

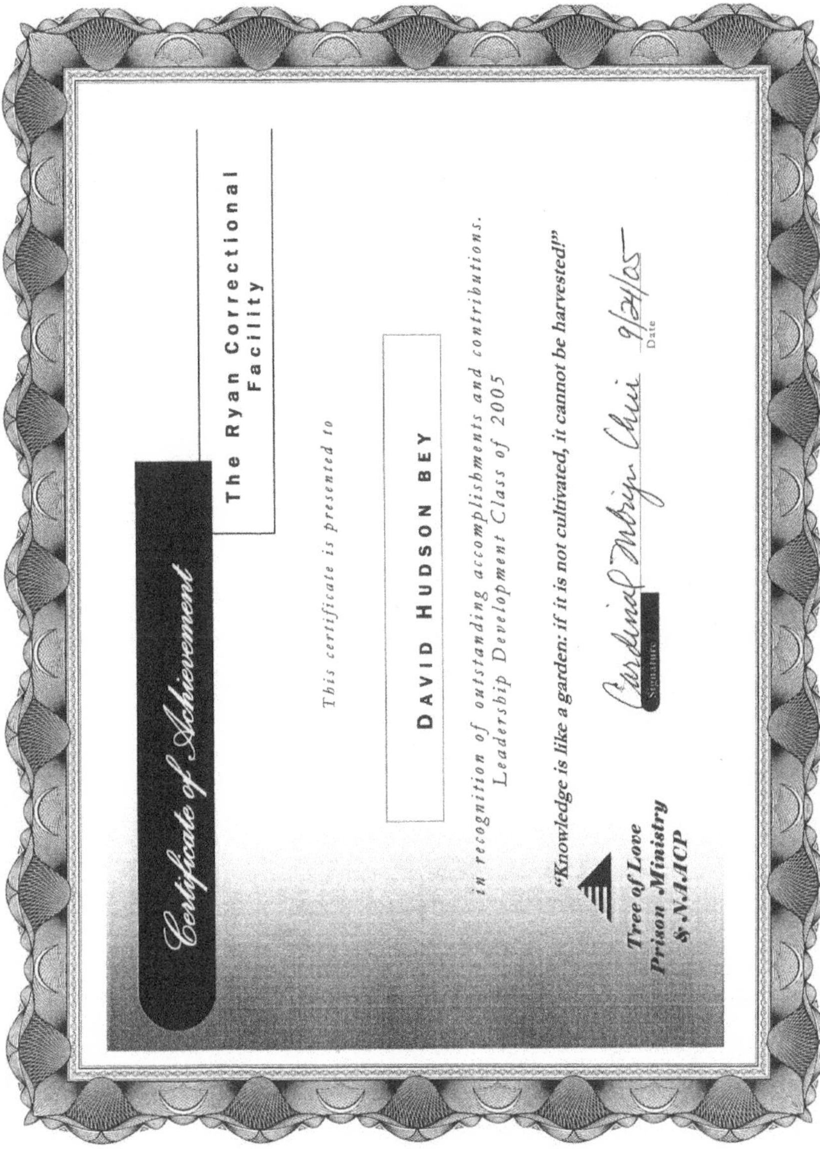

Certificate of Achievement

The Ryan Correctional Facility

This certificate is presented to

DAVID HUDSON BEY

in recognition of outstanding accomplishments and contributions.
Leadership Development Class of 2005

"Knowledge is like a garden: if it is not cultivated, it cannot be harvested!"

Signature

9/27/05
Date

Tree of Love
Prison Ministry
& N.A.A.C.P

Greater Detroit Michigan Chapter of Concerned Black Men, Inc

"...caring for our youth" ©

Certificate of Completion

presented to

David Hudson-Bey

In recognition of your completion of 30 *class hours of participation in our Male Responsibility & Fatherhood Development Program .*

We congratulate you for all you have accomplished.

Presented by:

Kenny Anderson

Kenny Anderson - Director

Dated: 9-24-05

STATE OF MICHIGAN
DEPARTMENT OF CORRECTIONS
LANSING

JENNIFER M. GRANHOLM
GOVERNOR

PATRICIA L. CARUSO
DIRECTOR

January 30, 2009

Tim Flanagan, Paralegal
Office of Legal Counsel
Office of Governor Jennifer M. Granholm
Romney Building, 1st Floor
111 S. Capitol Avenue
Lansing, Michigan 48933

RE: David Hudson #179401

Dear Mr. Flanagan:

The Parole Board sent an Application for Commutation of Sentence for the above referenced prisoner to the Office of Governor Granholm on December 12, 2008.

The attached letter was received from The Honorable Avern Cohn, United States District Court on September 26, 2008 and referred to Prisoner Hudson's Central Office file. Judge Cohn specifically asks in his letter that it be included in the report to the Governor on Hudson's petition. I would like to request that the letter be placed with the commutation application provided in December for consideration by Governor Granholm.

If you have any questions, please feel free to contact me.

Sincerely,

Amy Moore, Manager
Parole Board Lifer/Commutation Section

amm

GRANDVIEW PLAZA BUILDING • P.O. BOX 30003 • LANSING, MICHIGAN 48909
www.michigan.gov • (517) 335-1426

RICK SNYDER
GOVERNOR

STATE OF MICHIGAN
DEPARTMENT OF CORRECTIONS
LANSING

RICHARD M. McKEON
DIRECTOR

January 25, 2011

The Honorable Rick Snyder
Governor, State of Michigan
Attn: Cheri Arwood
Executive Administrator - Legal Division
George W. Romney Building
111 S. Capitol Avenue
Lansing, Michigan 48933

RE: Self-Initiated Application for Pardon or Commutation of Sentence
David Hudson, #179401
Lakeland Correctional Facility (LCF)
141 First Street
Coldwater, Michigan 49036

Dear Governor Snyder:

Attached is a copy of the Self-Initiated Application for Pardon or Commutation of Sentence filed by the above-named individual. This application is being submitted to you in accordance with the provisions of MCLA 791.244.

In compliance with the provisions of said statute, the Parole and Commutation Board has conducted a review of the application to determine if the request has merit.

By majority vote, the Parole and Commutation Board has determined that the application does **NOT** have merit and that Executive Clemency is not warranted. Therefore, denial of the application is recommended.

Respectfully submitted,

MICHIGAN PAROLE AND COMMUTATION BOARD

Barbara S. Sampson

Barbara Sampson, Chairperson

BSS:jld

Attachments

GRANDVIEW PLAZA • P.O. BOX 30003 • LANSING, MICHIGAN 48909
www.michigan.gov • (517) 335-1426

STATE OF MICHIGAN
DEPARTMENT OF CORRECTIONS
LANSING

K SNYDER
OVERNOR

DANIEL H. HEYNS
DIRECTOR

July 28, 2011

David Hudson, #179401
Lakeland Correctional Facility **(LCF)**
141 First Street
Coldwater, Michigan 49036

Dear Mr. Hudson:

Thank you for contacting the Michigan Parole Board.

During the commutation review process, the Parole Board takes into consideration several factors such as the nature and seriousness of the offense, any prior criminal history, the prisoner's institutional conduct, involvement in recommended programs, the potential for committing further assaultive or property crimes, and the prisoner's personal history and growth.

Your letter and the information you provided will be placed in your central office file so that Board members may take it into consideration in reviewing your case.

You will be scheduled for a lifer five (5) year file review on or about your Official Date of November 14, 2011.

Again, thank you for your letter.

Sincerely,

Michigan Parole Board

MPB/pab

PAROLE BOARD ACTION - EXECUTIVE SESSION

RE: SELF-INITIATED APPLICATION FOR PARDON OR COMMUTATION-CURRENT MICHIGAN PRISONER

INMATE NAME	INMATE NUMBER	DATE
David Hudson	**179401**	**September 7, 2010**

The Parole Board has determined the following regarding the above Self-Initiated Application for Pardon/ Commutation -- Current Michigan Prisoner

	Application **Has** Merit		Application Does **Not** Have Merit
Board Member	**Signature**	**Date**	**Signature**
1. Barbara S. Sampson			
2. James E. Atterberry		1/14/11	[signature]
3. Miguel Berrios			
4. Charles L. Brown		1/14/11	Charles Brown
5. Paul F. Condino		1/14/11	[signature]
6. Jodi DeAngelo		1/14/11	Jodi DeAngelo
7. Stephen H. DeBoer			
8. Ted Hammon		1/14/11	Ted Hammon
9. Robert Aguirre		1/14/11	Robert [signature]
10. Artina Tinsley Hardman		1/14/11	[signature]
11. Anthony King		01/14/11	Anthony E. O. King
12. David Kleinhardt			
13. John Sullivan		1/14/11	John Sullivan
14. Laurin' Thomas			
15. Sonia Warchock			

Date sent to Executive Session for discussion

Merit ________________ No Merit ________________

Note: Once all Members vote, the Application and attachments are to be returned to the Pardons and Commutations Coordinator.

MICHIGAN DEPARTMENT OF CORRECTIONS

PAROLE BOARD ACTION - EXECUTIVE SESSION

RE: SELF-INITIATED APPLICATION FOR PARDON OR COMMUTATION CURRENT MICHIGAN PRISONER

INMATE NAME	INMATE NUMBER	DATE
David Hudson	**179401**	**June 13, 2008**

The Parole Board has determined the following regarding the above Self-Initiated Application for Pardon/ Commutation -- Current Michigan Prisoner:

	Application Has Merit		Application Does Not Have Merit
Board Member	**Signature**	**Date**	**Signature**
1. Barbara S. Sampson		10/22/08	Barbara S. Sampson
2. James E. Atterberry		11/14/08	[illegible]
3. Miguel Berrios		10/28/08	[illegible]
4. Sharee Booker			
5. Stephen H. DeBoer		10/31/08	Stephen H. DeBoer
6. Artina Tinsley Hardman		12/1/08	[illegible]
7. Enid Livingston			
8. James J. Quinlan			
9. Laurin' Thomas	[illegible]	11/6/08	
10. David Kleinhardt (Acting)		11/24/08	[illegible]

Date sent to Executive Session for discussion

Merit ____________ No Merit ____________

Note: Once all Members vote, the Application and attachments are to be returned to the Pardons and Commutations Coordinator.

MICH. .AN DEPARTMENT OF CORR. .CTIONS

PAROLE BOARD ACTION - EXECUTIVE SESSION

RE: **SELF-INITIATED APPLICATION FOR PARDON OR COMMUTATION**
 CURRENT MICHIGAN PRISONER

INMATE NAME	INMATE NUMBER	DATE
David Hudson	**179401**	**March 31, 2004**

The Parole Board has determined the following regarding the above <u>Self-Initiated Application for Pardon/</u>
<u>Commutation -- Current Michigan Prisoner</u>:

Board Member	Application Has Merit Signature	Date	Application Does Not Have Merit Signature
1. John Rubitschun		4/13/04	*(signature)*
2. George Lellis		4/20/04	*(signature)*
3. Charles Braddock		4/12/04	*(signature)*
4. Miguel Berrios		4/13/04	*(signature)*
5. James E. Atterberry		4/19/04	*(signature)*
6. James J. Quinlan		4/13/04	*(signature)*
7. Margie R. McNutt		4/14/04	*(signature)*
8. Barbara S. Sampson		4/19/04	*(signature)*
9. Marianne Samper		4/12/04	*(signature)*
10. William A. Slaughter		4/12/04	*(signature)*

Date sent to Executive Session for discussion

Merit _____ No Merit _____

Note: Once all Members vote, the Application and attachments are to be returned to the Pardons and Commutations Coordinator

CORRECTIONS CODE OF 1953 (EXCERPT)
Act 232 of 1953

791.244 Parole board interview of prisoner serving sentence for first degree murder or sentence of imprisonment for life without parole; board duties upon own initiation or receipt of application for reprieve, commutation, or pardon; files as public record.

Sec. 44.

(1) Subject to the constitutional authority of the governor to grant reprieves, commutations, and pardons, 1 member of the parole board shall interview a prisoner serving a sentence for murder in the first degree or a sentence of imprisonment for life without parole at the conclusion of 10 calendar years and thereafter as determined appropriate by the parole board, until such time as the prisoner is granted a reprieve, commutation, or pardon by the governor, or is deceased. The interview schedule prescribed in this subsection applies to all prisoners to whom this section is applicable, regardless of when they were sentenced.

(2) Upon its own initiation of, or upon receipt of any application for, a reprieve, commutation, or pardon, the parole board shall do all of the following, as applicable:

(a) Not more than 60 days after receipt of an application, conduct a review to determine whether the application for a reprieve, commutation, or pardon has merit.

(b) Deliver either the written documentation of the initiation or the original application with the parole board's determination regarding merit, to the governor and retain a copy of each in its file, pending an investigation and hearing.

(c) Within 10 days after initiation, or after determining that an application has merit, forward to the sentencing judge and to the prosecuting attorney of the county having original jurisdiction of the case, or their successors in office, a written notice of the filing of the application or initiation, together with copies of the application or initiation, any supporting affidavits, and a brief summary of the case. Within 30 days after receipt of notice of the filing of any application or initiation, the sentencing judge and the prosecuting attorney, or their successors in office, may file information at their disposal, together with any objections, in writing, which they may desire to interpose. If the sentencing judge and the prosecuting attorney, or their successors in office, do not respond within 30 days, the parole board shall proceed on the application or initiation.

(d) If an application or initiation for commutation is based on physical or mental incapacity, direct the bureau of health care services to evaluate the condition of the prisoner and report on that condition. If the bureau of health care services determines that the prisoner is physically or mentally incapacitated, the bureau shall appoint a specialist in the appropriate field of medicine, who is not employed by the department, to evaluate the condition of the prisoner and to report on that condition. These reports are protected by the doctor-patient privilege of confidentiality, except that these reports shall be provided to the governor for his or her review.

(e) Within 270 days after initiation by the parole board or receipt of an application that the parole board has determined to have merit pursuant to subdivision (a), make a full investigation and determination on whether or not to proceed to a public hearing.

(f) Conduct a public hearing not later than 90 days after making a decision to proceed with consideration of a recommendation for the granting of a reprieve, commutation, or pardon. The public hearing shall be held before a formal recommendation is transmitted to the governor. One member of the parole board who will be involved in the formal recommendation may conduct the hearing, and the public shall be represented by the attorney general or a member of the attorney general's staff.

(g) At least 30 days before conducting the public hearing, provide written notice of the public hearing by mail to the attorney general, the sentencing trial judge, and the prosecuting attorney, or their successors in office, and each victim who requests notice pursuant to the crime victim's rights act, 1985 PA 87, MCL 780.751 to 780.834.

(h) Conduct the public hearing pursuant to the rules promulgated by the department. Except as otherwise provided in this subdivision, any person having information in connection with the pardon, commutation, or reprieve shall be sworn as a witness. A person who is a victim shall be given an opportunity to address and be questioned by the parole board at the hearing or to submit written testimony for the hearing. In hearing testimony, the parole board shall give liberal construction to any technical rules of evidence.

(i) Transmit its formal recommendation to the governor.

(j) Make all data in its files available to the governor if the parole board recommends the granting of a reprieve, commutation, or pardon.

(3) Except for medical records protected by the doctor-patient privilege of confidentiality, the files of the parole board in cases under this section shall be matters of public record.

History: 1953, Act 232, Eff. Oct. 2, 1953 ;-- Am. 1982, Act 314, Imd. Eff. Oct. 15, 1982 ;-- Am. 1992, Act 181, Imd. Eff. Sept. 22, 1992 ;-- Am. 1999, Act 191, Eff. Mar. 10, 2000
Popular Name: Department of Corrections Act
Admin Rule: R 791.1101 et seq. of the Michigan Administrative Code.

RESOURCES

BOOKS

Amstutz, Lorraine Stutzman. *Victim Offender Conferencing*
ISBN978-1-56148-586-4

Carter, Les. *The Anger Trap*
ISBN-10: 078796879X; ISBN-13: 978-0787968793

Casarjian, Robin. *Houses of Healing*
ISBN 0-9644933

Engel, Beverly. *Women Circling the Earth: A Guide to Fostering Community, Healing, and Empowerment.* (Deerfield Beach, Florida: Health Communications, 2000)

Freeman-Longo, Robert E., & Bays, Laren. *Enhancing Empathy*
ISBN-10:1929657048; ISBN-13:978-1929657049

Goleman, Daniel. *Emotional Intelligence*
ISBN-10: 0555380491X; ISBN-13: 978-0553804911

Goleman, Daniel. *Social Intelligence*
ISBN-10: 055338449X; ISBN-13: 978-0553384499

Kivel, Paul. *Men's Work*
ISBN-1: 56868-233-2

Lozoff, Bo, & the Dalai Lama. *We're All Doing Time: A Guide to Getting Free*
ISBN-10:0961444401; ISBN-13: 978-0961444402

Millman, Dan. *Way of the Peaceful Warrior*
ISBN-10: 1932073256; ISBN-13: 978-1932073256

Samenow, Stanton E. *Inside the Criminal Mind*
ISBN-978-1-4000-4619-5

Yochelson, Samuel, & Samenow, Staton E. *The Criminal Personality*
ISBN-978-1-56823-349-1

SELECT YOUTH REFERENCES

Alexander Youth Services
Center
Charles Waddell, Director
1502 Woody Drive
Alexander, AR 72002

Arise Foundation
824 US Highway One
Suite 240
North Palm Beach, FL 33408
Phone: (888) 860-6100

Augusta Youth Development
Campus
Edna May-Wiggins, Director
3481 Mike Padgett Highway
Augusta, GA 30906

Boys to Men Group Home
750 E. Pine St.
Compton, CA 90221
Phone: (310) 608-1007

Bureau for at Risk Youth Inc.
155 Dupont St.
Plainview, NY 11803
Phone: (516) 576-3094

Catholic Youth Organization
920 S. Broad St.
Trenton, NJ 08611
(609) 396-8383

City Wide Youth Leadership
Agency
1021 Ridge Avenue Fl 4
Philadelphia, PA 19123
Phone: (215) 765-5504

Davis Center
Blackwater Falls Rd.
Davis, WV 262260

Deter Me Not Girls
Youth Group
1523 N 99th St.
Los Angeles, CA 90047
Phone: (323) 753-4457

Echo Glen Children's Center
33010 SE 99th St.
Snoqualmire, WA 98065

Homesburg Boys Club
7756 Dutman St.
Philadelphia, PA 19136
Phone: (215) 338-0733

Judge Greg Mathis
Community Center
19300 Greenfield
Detroit, MI 48235
(313) 342-8582

Kids Off The Block
11621 South Michigan
Avenue #1
Chicago, IL 60628

Life Directions Peers
5716 Michigan Ave.
Suite 2200
Detroit, MI 48210

Living Arts
8701 W. Vernor Suite 202
Detroit, MI 48209
Phone: (313) 841-4765

Michigan Fla Shawono Center
10 N. Howes Lake Rd.
Grayling, MI 40738

Mountview Youth Services
Center
Penny Brown, Director
3900 S. Carr St.
Denver, CO 80235

National Guard Youth
Foundation
1001 N. Fairfax St., Suite 205
Alexandria, VA 22314
Phone: (703) 684-5437

New York Youth At Risk
25 W. 36th St. #8
New York, NY 10018
Phone: (212) 791-4927

Oakland Schools Homeless
Student
Education Program
2214 Mall Drive E.
Waterford, MI 48328
Phone: (248) 209-2430

Outward Bound
2582 Riceville Rd.
Asheville, NC 28805
Phone: (866) 467-7651

Positive Action Community
Service
1620 W. Stiles St.
Philadelphia, PA 19121
Phone: (215) 684-2737
Southern Oaks Girls School
21425 B Spring St.
Union Grove, WI 54442-9720

Uplift Our Youth Foundation
Randall Talifarro, Vice
Chairman
POB 70099
Lansing, MI 48908
(517) 285-9373

Variety Boys' and Girls' Club
1300 Plaza del Sol St.
Los Angeles, CA 90033
Phone: (323) 266-0409

Youth Group Gallery
19 Hope St.
Brooklyn, NY 11211
Phone: (718) 384-4222

Youthville Detroit
7375 Woodward
Detroit, MI 48202
Phone: (313) 309-1300

JOB CORP CENTERS

Detroit Job Corps Center
11801 Woodrow Wilson St.
Detroit, MI 48206

Grand Rapids Job Corps Center
110 Hall St. S.E.
Grand Rapids, MI 49507

Flint Job Corps Center
2400 N. Saginaw St.
Flint, MI 48505

GANGSTA GLOSSARY

Burner Gun, pistol, rifle, automatic weapon.
Carried by 6 Funeral proceedings; having your casket carried by six pallbearers; to get killed.
Catch a Case To be caught and charged with a felony (retail fraud, larceny, robbery, car jacking, home invasion, murder).
Eight-fee 8 ounces of cocaine, crack; **big eight** is 8½ ounces of cocaine or crack.
Flags Gang symbols, such as bandannas or hand gestures.
Flip Top Box Casket for a funeral.
Flipping Selling for a profit; exchanging items or products for currency or for items of equal or greater value (drug sales, stolen cars or parts, etc.).
Four-O's—and a Baby 4½ ounces of cocaine; 28 grams per ounce; illegal street drugs, crack, heroine.
Game or **This Game** A particular lifestyle or street life hustle; the drug game, the pimp game, etc.; code or rules outside of society's norms.
Gangsta 1) a member of a rural or urban street gang; 2) a performer of gangsta rap; 3) a street hustler that would do most anything for money; 4) an intelligent student who desires the elusive glory of hot girls, expensive cars, jewelry, and popping bottles without completing his education.
Judged by 12 Criminal jury trial; court proceedings with a judge presiding over a jury; 12 law abiding citizens sitting on jury duty. The street phase "I'd rather be judged by 12 than carried by six" means I would rather kill than be killed, or I would rather shoot than be shot.

Juvie Juvenile; Juvenile Detention Center; Crimes committed by children under the age of 17 years old; 17-year-old street thug; Young gangsta; a minor engaged in street crime.

Maslow Hierarchy of Needs Most basic are physiological needs for air, food, water, and sleep. Next are fundamental security needs: shelter, health, safety, companions, employment, and property. When these needs are met people seek love and belonging (friendship, intimacy, family, trust) and then esteem (respect, accomplishment, self-confidence). At the highest level in Maslow's pyramid is what he called self-actualization, the pursuit and realization of one's core values—becoming what one is meant to be.

Misconducts Prison write-ups; tickets; equal to a felony in society (e.g., being in the wrong place without permission, getting caught with drugs, weapons, or cell phone; fighting, stabbing, theft, etc., while in prison).

Murkin Season Period of time when large numbers of homicides typically occur (e.g., summertime, the start of the school year, holiday season).

Quick Dollar Illegal street money; drug money; the sale of illegal goods for money; money earned illegally or unethically.

Re-copping Selling drugs, turning a profit to buy more drugs in an equal or greater quantity. Buying illegal drugs.

Scrub Street Hustler Someone not well educated in the street code of making money. A newcomer to drugs, streets, pimping, stealing, or other illegal activities. Working for someone else and taking most of the risk for little or minimum profit; a front-line hustler; someone visibly on the street corner selling illegally.

Strapped Carrying a gun or pistol; having a concealed weapon on your person or body.

Spud Juice Homemade wine in prison: stolen items combined from correctional facility food service (e.g., a combination of orange juice, sugar, yeast or some other type of fruit juices), fermented to alcohol-like substance (generally 3-10%).

Wangsta Person who pretends to be streetwise or a "Gangsta," but who, when put to the test, freezes up or cooperates with the police by turning on his crime partner(s).

CPSIA information can be obtained
at www.ICGtesting.com
Printed in the USA
FFHW020217131218
49866129-54431FF

9 781490 732640